Overcome Your Storm, Rebuild Your Hope

Rodney Bennett

# OVERCOME YOUR STORM, REBUILD YOUR HOPE

## Rodney Bennett

**Foreword By:**
Rev. Dr. Hilda J. Covington

Redemption's Story Publishing, LLC, Houston, Texas (USA)

Overcome Your Storm, Rebuild Your Hope

Overcome Your Storm, Rebuild Your Hope

Copyright © 2020
Rodney Bennett

All Rights Reserved.
No portion of this publication may be reproduced, stored in an electronic system, or transmitted in any form or by any means (electronic, mechanical, photocopy, recording, or otherwise) without written permission from the author or publisher. Brief quotations may be used in literary reviews.

Print ISBN 13: 978-1-948853-12-5
Digital ISBN 13: 978-1-948853-13-2
Library of Congress Control Number: 2020948530

**For information and bulk ordering, contact:**
*Redemption's Story Publishing, LLC*
Angela Edwards, CEO
P.O. Box 62287
Houston, TX 77205
RedeemedByHim@Redemptions-Story.com

## What Others Are Saying...

*"This is a beautiful, amazing testimony [true story] of how God will turn it all around – of how our 'mess' becomes the 'message.' This is a must-read for those who are in these phases of life."*
**~ Pastor Joseph A. Bishop ~**
Associate Pastor of Victory Outreach Church of North Philadelphia

\*\*\*\*\*\*\*\*\*\*

*"This book is a must-read for anyone facing hardships and adversity. Rev. Rodney Bennett (RodneyBSpeaks) is an overcomer who is equipped to help others navigate their way through the storms of life."*
**~ Pastor Joy Morgan~**
Author, *Roadmap to Destiny: A 21-Day Devotional for Those on the Pathway to Purpose* and *G.E.T. U.P.: 5 Steps to Bouncing Back When Life Knocks You Down*

\*\*\*\*\*\*\*\*\*\*

*"In* Overcome Your Storm, Rebuild Your Hope, *Rodney Bennett inspires you to take ownership of the pre-existent value that God Himself has wired into you and by which He speaks to you, through the dreams and passions of your history, your present, and YES, your future."*
**~ W. Wayne Holmes ~**
Rodney's Former Pastor and Friend
Prison Chaplain and Seminar Speaker

\*\*\*\*\*\*\*\*\*\*

"*Overcome Your Storm, Rebuild Your Hope is filled with words spoken from the heart of one who has endured much and then overcame many obstacles and abysses in life. The message of hope permeates each paragraph, takes root, and grows until the anticipation of victory in the reader's life bursts forth from the pages. Although there are no guarantees in life, Rodney Bennett (aka RodneyBSpeaks) shows that with God, nothing is impossible.*"

~ **Cassandra Ulrich** ~

Author, *A Beautiful Girl*

Youth Group Volunteer at First Baptist Church of Haddonfield and Revolution Youth at Oaklyn Baptist Church

http://cassandraulrich.com

# Dedication

This book is dedicated to my mom, **Constance Naomi Bennett**, and my hero, my dad, who recently lost his battle with cancer. My parents have **Hollie Bennett** been twin mountains of inspiration, correction, love, and faith in the Lord Jesus Christ and have made me the man I am today. Before his transition, my dad spoke of sitting on a bench in Heaven, talking with his father and me about the goodness of the Lord. Wow! I can't wait! Save my seat, daddy! I love you very much, Mom and Dad.

This is also dedicated to my beautiful ride-or-die sisters, **Kim Harris and Donna Finney**. They have seen me at my absolute worst, yet they never ceased to believe God for a miracle for me. They loved me, even when they hated what I was doing. Unlike any other, they watched and felt the ricochet effects of pain and disappointment from the man I used to be. I'm so glad they are here to see the beginning of a new journey as I now head in the opposite direction. I love you both very much.

## Special Appreciation

Some days, I feel like I'm on the ocean riding jet skis between two lighthouses. I have been so fortunate in my life. I have always had exceptional people around me who double-dared me not to aspire to do and be the same. Presently, my life is bookended by two individuals who have provided support and light.

Special appreciation is given to these wonderful sisters. I respect their visions, their shepherding, their wisdom, their education (Doctorates), and their drive. Also noteworthy is they have both battled serious illnesses over their lifetimes. I'm sure their respective sicknesses realized they made a mistake when they chose to mess with these two.

- ❖ For almost ten years, Pastor Hilda Covington has guided me, taught me, and loved me into the birth of a new ministry.
- ❖ For a little over a year, Pastor Joy Morgan has inspired, modeled, coached, and empowered me into a new destiny.

Thank you both very, very much.

I also want to give a very special appreciation to two people who relentlessly encouraged me and believed in me the entire time I was writing this book: my daughter, Kelly Anderson, and my friend and the administrator of our church, Evangelist Linda Burkett. Unbeknownst to them, they would sometimes take turns nudging me to keep it moving, no matter what. Amazingly, they've never met and live miles apart! Thank you, ladies! We did it!

# Acknowledgments

I want first to thank Mr. Carlos Brown-Bey and his wife, Rev. Olive Brown-Bey, who preceded him to Glory. Almost ten years ago, they gathered together a group of leaders from Victory Outreach Church in Washington, DC. As successful business owners, they inspired and unleashed us to pursue entrepreneurship to support our families and the ministry, led by Pastors Chuck and Lavenise Turner. Thanks, Big Bro. It worked!

To Dr. AJ Rolls, Success Resurrector: Almost eight years ago, you envisioned this in me. You shared with me your experience as a successful author of 12 books and a professional presenter. You challenged me to write, speak, and tell my story, so I did! Thanks, man. I couldn't have done it without you.

I am eternally grateful for the small treasure chest of accomplished authors who invited me into their inner circle, "The Legends Group": Ken Snowden, Cassandra Ulrich, Margaret Brown, Steve Bucelli, Steve Baker, and Tracy Taylor: There, they taught me the mechanics of critiquing, editing, and crafting my writing, along with some tips on the business side. In its early stages, they helped me critique this book. Thank you all for your support.

Lastly, I wish to acknowledge someone very special from my youth: my high school English teacher at Burlington Township High School, Mrs. Vivian Kurilla (deceased). I will never forget her. She continually snatched me out of class and corrected my childish shenanigans, all while insisting there was greatness inside of me. She wanted me to pursue a career as a political journalist, which I thought was preposterous. I never did understand what she saw in me…until now. Thank you for everything, Mrs. Kurilla.

# Foreword

When someone picks up a manual, there is an assumption that there is a need to know, a desire to learn how to get better or conquer and move past the situation that has them bound. For some, understanding takes years. For others, it is merely a flick of a switch that causes light to break forth to eradicate all their darkness and insecurities. It is as if they suddenly see a way out.

The year is 2020. It is now public record that there is an epidemic in the land — one of gargantuan proportions in every city, every state, and every country.

Hurting people — no matter the source of pain — just don't want to hurt anymore.

We have confused the sacred promise of perfect peace in the Holy Bible with our desire for "no pain." We are seeking "no more hurt" rather than "more peace."

The opioid crisis in our country today is one of the issues that has evolved because of man's constant quest to alight on the shores of a place with no pain. This "manual" lets us know there is no such place and that *"advancing through adversity is a process and not a sprint; so, don't time it — endure it!"*

In this book, Rev. Rodney Bennett reminds us that we will find evidence of new growth on the inside after each storm in our lives. In his "Seven Laws of Advancing Through Adversity," he demonstrates a focus or an attribute necessary for us to move through to victory. His visualizations of the process steps are unique to him and the reality of how God can inspire each of us with both clarity and simplicity.

Rodney Bennett

Almost 40 years ago, I was one of the people his mother requested to pray with her for her son. I have bore witness to many of the storms he speaks of and can attest to his process.

As humans, we are often hindered when we highlight a step in the process while failing to completely identify real adversity. Hence, the lesson is lost, and we will repeat the class.

That is why Rev. Bennett is a member of the Pastoral team at Wayside Community Church and Director of "The Cure" — our outreach program addressing those caught up in addictions of any kind. He is also a member of the Board of Directors for SisterHood Incorporated — a community-based and international nonprofit organization.

What a blessing it is to release a written word from the heart! This is a word that has been entrusted to you alone, Rev. Bennett, to bring increase just when the world needs it.

Rev. Bennett has, indeed, brought increase to us all through this manual of hope. It is essential to note that he has recounted his personal experiences in such a way that others can identify (in whole or part) and be helped by them.

The experience of overcoming our storms and recognizing and developing the tools needed to rebuild our hope needs to be shared. Rodney has done that most excellently! Having come this far, read on! When you have finished, I decree and declare that you will be empowered and encouraged to take a leap of faith and advance through whatever level life's adversity is calling you to.

*~ Rev. Dr. Hilda J. Covington ~*

# Preface

*A Process.* About seven years ago, I relocated back to New Jersey from Washington, DC. While in DC, I had the privilege of serving as a leader in a worldwide movement called "Victory Outreach International." Then, I was back in New Jersey.

I remember sitting in my basement, seriously contemplating a career change. I had several trades to fall back on. I recently had been employed as a pipeline technician (or pipefitter), working on underground gas lines in DC. That kind of work was lucrative but very dangerous. Considering the new responsibility level that accompanied my new family, we decided that line of work was not the best option.

We all have our own form of coping and processing mechanisms—good and bad. My most frequently used is prayer and meditation.

While I prayed that day in the basement, I remember thinking of the account of an older woman in the Bible who had a tremendous financial obligation due to the recent death of her husband. She poured out her complaint to a prophet by the name of Isaiah. His response to her was in the form of a question: *"What do you have in your house?"* She said, *"Nothing, except this little bowl of cooking oil."* She was then told all she had was all she needed. That oil was miraculously multiplied by God. She then sold it, paid her bills, and lived on the rest.

I felt like that elderly lady. "Except for my oil" represented my life story or "testimony." But how could this be fulfilled? By telling it!

I rushed off to talk to the one person I knew who was doing that kind of thing: a respected cousin of mine (AJ) who is a professional presenter. *"Write a book,"* he advised. While on my job at Purato's, Inc.—a food manufacturing plant in Cherry Hill, New Jersey, where I am still employed—I wrote during every break, after work, before bed, and even when on vacation.

This book is the beginning of "The Oil."

***A People.*** After writing for some time, I began to think, *"To whom am I writing?"* There is a group of people I seem to connect with and ignite to act consistently. Many of us have success with impacting the lives of people we have the most in common with. That has always been the case with me. I almost always identify with and gravitate towards those who have a past like mine: addiction—especially if my past looks more like their present.

Something very interesting and amazing happened to me while in DC. I fell in love and bonded with a group of young people from the city's Southeast section. However, none of them were like me when I was their age. I couldn't explain it at first but soon realized that I possessed a strong desire to work with young people internally. I loved being around them. I went to their schools, met their parents, and helped them with their homework. I even assisted them with picking and unpicking boyfriends or girlfriends. I broke up fights and taxied a few of them to supermarkets and to shop for school clothes. Sadly, one of the young men lost his life to gun violence one night after a group of them left my apartment.

After earning the youth's trust and their parents, the kids opened up to me and allowed me to walk with them through their joys and pains. That was one of the most valuable experiences I have had in my life. All this time later, I remain in contact with many of them today.

*A Passion.* After resettling in New Jersey, I continued to write and reflect on my time in DC. I began listening to and reading about young people in my home state of New Jersey and across the United States.

One issue seemed to arrest my attention: suicide. It tore apart families, schools, and communities. I wondered if there was anything I could do to help.

One day while researching, I came across a bombshell that triggered something deep inside my soul. The statistic stated the number one cause of suicide was hopelessness. Yet another stated hopelessness was the second leading cause of death among young people.

That was it!

*"I have been through so much adversity in my life. There is one thing I can easily give to anyone, and that is* **HOPE***,"* I thought. So, I endeavored to upgrade hope to a platinum level.

This book marks the beginning of a new breed of hope in one of the most hopeless times in our history—right now!

Platinum Hope is here!

**NOTE:** *University of Adversity classes will begin soon.*

Rodney Bennett

# **Introduction**

*The Portrait... A True Story*

The loud steel screech of the subway brakes is heard as we advance from station to station. Returning from a business trip, I inch closer to home. The usual public transportation aromas are strangely absent from this subway car. The vibrating, shifting feeling of the train rolling on the tracks seems to be a unique lullaby.

Then, it happens.

My eyelids quickly glide down over my eyes, and the open door to a much-needed rest closes behind me. Fifty-four seconds whisk past. I then hear a voice at the entrance of this serene room in which I am now reclining. It is the front right side of my brain, saying, *"Hey, you're going to miss your stop if you don't wake up."* As if hearing a hypnotist snap his fingers, I spring back to the real world.

*"Where am I?"* I blurt out. My readjusting eyes reply, *"You are still on the subway."*

Sometimes while on the train, if I'm not studying or checking emails, I pass the time by reading the advertisement panels located above our heads in the train car.

My eyes are somehow drawn to the couple sitting in the seats across from mine, divided by a thin gray aisle. The distance between us is no more than six feet. He sits next to her, closest to the window. I remember glancing at the number of the train operator placed over an entrance: Number 269. Then, I briefly glance back over to the couple. It's as if a portrait has been hung before me.

## Overcome Your Storm, Rebuild Your Hope

They are a couple…two people…together…close and connected.

She sits closest to the gray side and strikes a confident pose. Her sleek, neatly-styled hair is draped over her shoulders. She wears some sort of collared shirt with a black jacket. Her modest dark blue jeans suggest an image of relaxation. Two features stand out slightly from the rest of this young woman's appearance. Her boots are stylish—below the knee but above the calf and made of suede…the smoothest, softest, coolest member of the clothing fabric family. The boots neatly overlap the jeans, tucked into them. These boots look as if they are contoured around the shape of her legs and feet. They were probably costly and relatively new. The shade of her footwear was an endlessly deep, rich, charcoal black.

Clearly, however, the most notable aspect of this woman's appearance was her face. Although I could only see her from one side, her thoughts' weight was obviously cumbersome while her lips were silent. Etched in my mind was the stare on her face. Her gaze said, *"I am frustrated!"* I could feel her stare. It was anger. It was regret. It was motionlessly fixed. This woman was dressed modestly and took care of herself, but her look seemed incompatible with the rest of her demeanor.

Then, with 4G-like speed, I made a connection!

As I glanced directly at her, trying not to be discourteous or intrusive, it hit me: her partner was high, although she was not. When I say "high," I mean he was sailing in the wind like an old box kite.

There sat a couple, two close and connected people, except one of them is frantic, treading toxic water and gasping for breath, but slowly sinking into the deep, gloomy swamp of addiction. He chose heroin—a weapon of mass destruction. I've seen people under the influence of this narcotic before. I am all too familiar with the body language, the swerving in and out of consciousness, the scratching, the glazed look in the eyes, and the keen awareness of their surroundings, even during the part of the euphoric feeling a heroin addict experiences known as "the nod" or "the groove."

Actually, this one dark, thought-provoking portrait was two portraits in one frame: his addiction and her affliction. Nevertheless, a portrait is now hanging before me. This is a couple—two people, together, close and connected. They are a portrait…of a severe storm of adversity.

Yet, there is ***Hope***.

Overcome Your Storm, Rebuild Your Hope

# Table of Contents

What Others Are Saying… ....................................................................... vi

Dedication ................................................................................................ viii

Special Appreciation ................................................................................ ix

Acknowledgments ..................................................................................... x

Foreword ................................................................................................... xi

Preface ..................................................................................................... xiii

Introduction ............................................................................................. xvi

**Part 1: Overcome Your Storm** .............................................................. 1

    Chapter One – What Is Adversity ............................................................ 2

    Chapter Two – The Benefits of Adversity ............................................. 15

    Chapter Three – Breakdown or Breakthrough? ..................................... 27

    Chapter Four – P.O.W. (Prisoner of War) .............................................. 34

    Chapter Five – How to Win Against Adversity ..................................... 49

    Chapter Six – Seven Laws of Advancing Through Adversity ............... 61

**Part 2: Rebuild Your Hope** .................................................................. 67

    Chapter Seven – What Is Hope? ............................................................ 68

Chapter Eight – The Value of Hope ..................................................... 75

Chapter Nine – Rebuild Your Hope After the Storms of Adversity ...... 83

Chapter Ten – The Dream Team ........................................................... 93

Chapter Eleven – Grown-Up Hope Is A Realized Dream .................... 103

Chapter Twelve – Just Can't Imagine ................................................. 111

About the Author ................................................................................ 116

# Part 1:
# Overcome Your Storm

Rodney Bennett

# Chapter One
# What Is Adversity?

What is 'adversity'? Adversity is something we all must face. At its core, it is defined as "misfortune, calamity, trouble, or disaster." Even though we experience adversity, there is no reason we cannot continue to move forward.

Adversity does not have to make you adverse. Adverse denotes moving or working in an opposite or contrary direction. Remember how challenging life has been at times. You have had to punch, kick, and do everything else to survive some of life's ultimate cage-fighting wars. Some were within; some were without. You have battled with both people and apparitions. Many of your conflicts were in your own head.

I know what I'm talking about because I, too, have had a few clashes with the past that have left me with a loose tooth or two.

Some of us have had to reach down into the soil of our own hearts. There, we found words attaching like weeds — cluttering, choking, and robbing us of the rich garden that should have been growing. When the weeds were removed and replaced, we are now vibrant and full of life.

What gives adversity the right to barbarically barge into our lives and stomp on our dreams, visions, and hope into the ground? Well, that, my friend, is what this book is all about!

You will see it is possible to move past adversity and move on with your life, all while being enriched by its curriculum. Adversity will measure you. Adversity is where you really learn what kind of person you are on the inside. Adversity can be one of the most skilled teachers that exist—if you decide to be its pupil.

Sometimes, we stop progress as adversity approaches. One reason we quit is that we have yet to decide to pursue something at all costs.

I once heard a story about an old preacher and a young man. The young man came to the old preacher and told him he, too, would one day be a preacher. The older, wiser man said to the young man, *"You are not going to be a preacher."* A person who overheard those words was shocked and thought it was extremely insensitive for the older preacher to respond that way. Later, that same person found out the old preacher had encountered many young men over the years in that same situation. Throughout his years, the preacher had learned that if he could talk them out of that idea, then they probably didn't really want it or deserve it. Periodically, there would be someone who could not and would not be denied. They would threaten to leave the office and the church, too, in order to pursue their goal. They were the right ones for the job.

The moral of the story is this: When adversity attacks your dreams, it will show you how much you really want what you say you want.

There's an adage that says, *"If you fall apart when adversity comes, your strength is not very great."* One of the ideas conveyed in the word 'strength' is the power to resist force or pressure. Your physical muscles become strong as you resist the weight and pressure being exerted against that muscle. Overcoming adversity is a lot like lifting weights. Your ability and desire to push against the force of misfortune will develop your inner muscles.

Do you understand that you have strength internally as well as externally? That is to say, you can develop strength of mind and soul as tangibly as you can build density in your triceps and quadriceps. In fact, it is really that internal strength that has the most effect on your external self.

For example, as a beginner in weightlifting, you can't really tell how strong you are. The way you know your true power is to see how much weight your muscles can resist. I used to love hearing the ear-ringing "clang" as one of my workout buddies slammed another 45-pound plate on each side of the solid steel bar used to hold the avalanche of iron that would undoubtedly cause my muscles to bake even more than the last set…

Oh. I'm sorry. Where was I?

Have you ever been in a place in your life where it felt like everything was on cruise control? You may have been at school, home, on your job, or at the park, and everything was smooth sailing. Then suddenly, things changed.

I remember growing up many years ago in my old neighborhood, LaGorce Square. Growing up there was like a real version of a TV sports center. There was always something happening. Within the community, there were multiple cultures. Various games and sports were played as well—often happening all at once. I recall the football team rivalries: "Your Street vs. My Street," "Your Section vs. My Section," and so on. At a place we simply referred to as "the courts," there were babies, little kids, teens, and middle-aged individuals present regularly. There were males and females—players, spectators, and coaches. Also, there were visitors from Burlington City, Florence, and Willingboro communities, many of whom were top high school athletes at the time. There were baseball, softball, football, boxing, weight training, chess, horseshoes, cookouts, and even block parties in the warmer months. At all times, though—even in the winter—*there was basketball.*

By now, you are likely thinking, *"Wasn't Rodney just talking about the definition of adversity?"* Please keep reading...

"The courts" consisted of two full-length basketball courts, a baseball diamond, a few picnic tables, a small playground, and a couple of grills, with a huge water tower that stood nearby, proudly displaying its nametag: Burlington Township. In that space, it was not uncommon to see two or three games being played simultaneously. Sometimes, I played basketball and was probably one level beneath 'average.' But, if my boys and I hustled up to the court as soon as middle school was out, we could usually find a half- or full-court open. That was the time when just us sixth and seventh graders could shine. We razzled, and we dazzled. We dribbled between our legs and passed behind our backs. We shot rainbow jump shots (this was before three-pointers) and last-minute buzzer-beaters. We shone like new silver dollars.

*But...*

As time went on, we knew that every day like clockwork, sooner or later, we would hear those very familiar show-ending words:

**"WE GOT NEXT!"**

Those words seemed to reverberate throughout our outdoor multiplex arena like a huge church bell before Sunday school. Those very words meant things were about to change.

You see, generally speaking, when playing street, park, or playground-level sports, the term *"WE GOT NEXT"* is very clear. It usually means something like:

*"We have checked out your team and the one you're playing against. We have made mental notes of each team's strengths and weaknesses. We also understand that on both teams, there are exceptional players. We think we have assessed your team and have individuals who can match or surpass their skill level."*

In a nutshell, whichever team wins, they are confident they will thoroughly embarrass "NEXT."

However, at our level of youth play, the words *"WE GOT NEXT"* (as spoken from the older, more experienced players) meant:

*"Take your ball and dribble on the sidelines until tomorrow because WE are getting ready to take over the whole court."*

Once in a while, we courageously responded to *"WE GOT NEXT"* with *"WE GOT FIVE."* That meant we were already on the court, so we have the first opportunity to challenge the opposing team, which is basketball etiquette and protocol. For us, when we uttered those words, it was usually the sum of adversity. We didn't have poise, skill, persistence, or any other qualifications needed to succeed. All we had to our credit was the ability to imitate what we saw on television, along with a thimbleful of talent.

What is my point, you ask? Well, here it is:

When the word "NEXT" was said, we knew the level of play had shifted drastically. If we did get a chance to play, we would be harassed, wounded, verbally abused, and challenged every second. Most of the time, we were clearly outmatched — unless, of course, the older guys had consumed several beers before their arrival, which was rare.

Sometimes, I would say to myself, *"Dang, man! I was a superstar a half-hour ago!"*

Have you ever experienced a time in your life when you shined, thrived, razzled, and dazzled until someone more competent and skilled came along? You may have felt you wanted to compete, but it also related to what you sometimes encounter while overcoming the storms of adversity. How? Because in the same way we collided with the older, more experienced athletes when we were kids, encountering a sudden storm of adversity can be intimidating. You may feel a lack of confidence in your ability to compete against your 'competitor.' With a twinge of uncertainty, you ask yourself, *"Am I ready for this? Am I strong enough? Have I actually faced anything like this before?"* You might also think, *"Can I endure this? Can I ultimately last over the span of time this storm will be present, or will it become too overwhelming?"*

Here's the good news: If you can harness the courage and self-discipline you have, it is possible to resist the temptation to be fearful. You can rise to another level. You can become better. Today, adversity may be harassing, mentally abusing, and challenging you on every side, but you will become a different person as you advance through it skillfully.

So many times in life, we want to achieve specific goals. The problem is we don't know what awaits us as we travel down that road. We don't know what the journey will really cost us. Adversity can be misleading sometimes because it seems as if you can't see anything valuable that can come out of it while going through. One true reason is that we are so prone to classifying our experiences by what we feel. If we feel bad, then it must be a bad experience. We don't often consider the good a particularly negative experience can produce in us. I know some may disagree, but feelings and emotions are not always the best barometers by which to govern our decisions. Conscience and reason will serve us much better.

Now that adversity has been defined, let's make sure we have a few things we will need on this road trip as we "Overcome Adversity and Rebuild Hope."

There are three skills I believe will be invaluable as you journey toward your destiny. I have put together a simple analogy that may help you understand and remember them. The names of the three attributes are:

- **Hindsight**
- **Foresight**
- **Insight**

As you travel, think of hindsight as a rearview mirror. It allows you to see what is behind you. Imagine that foresight is your windshield. It enables you to see what is ahead. Finally, insight is like your headlights. It empowers you when you can't clearly see your way. The rearview mirror, windshield, and headlights are three features necessary in driving an automobile safely.

## *Hindsight*

Loosely defined, hindsight is when you recognize something after its occurrence. So, if you were driving, there are some things you would recognize after you pass them.

As you digest the topic of adversity, it is essential to learn from your experiences. In fact, if you look closely, there are likely layers of important lessons you can peel and learn from that will assist you as you progress. Make a notation of the lessons you have learned in life because they will be of great importance as you grow. However, as you advance, don't look too long in your rearview mirror, as you just may end up in a cornfield. Just glance back periodically while remaining primarily focused on where you are going.

During your lifetime, you will experience many seasons of adversity. But, as you master new skills and mindsets, you can navigate through those storms more efficiently. You will also be able to remain focused on your hopes, dreams, and visions. Hindsight is seeing and understanding things you have already passed.

Imagine yourself driving down a scenic country road. You pass mountains and tall, beautiful trees in that landscape. As you pass by, it is interesting to see them from a different perspective — the rearview mirror. What would driving be like without that mirror? After you passed by something, you would no longer be able to see it. What if you saw a pedestrian fall as you were driving by? Without a rearview mirror, you wouldn't be able to see if they were alright. Instead, you would have to pull over to the shoulder of the road.

Similarly, if you passed a car accident, the rearview mirror could assist you. While you could just turn around, you might instinctively look in the rearview mirror because you know it's there. It is convenient and valuable.

Life without hindsight is like driving without using your rearview mirror. You would feel as if you're missing out on something you know you have. Unlike an automobile, however, I believe people are born with the hindsight skill that must be sharpened by being exercised.

Learn to be a student in the class as you study YOU! Try to understand what makes you 'tick,' but don't be overly judgmental or cynical. Don't be afraid to learn from your life. The more studious you become in the 'class of you,' the easier it can be to move forward. You may not do it immediately, but find the strength to gradually pull over to the side of the road to take a long, hard look at the issues you have passed by with the intention of personal growth.

Ask yourself questions along the way, such as, *"How did this happen? Am I alone responsible? Has serious damage occurred? Am I ready to move on?"* The answers may not always come to you easily because the responses may hurt, but discipline yourself to use your "rearview mirror" or hindsight.

## *Foresight*

Think of foresight as your windshield. It relates to knowledge gained by looking forward as you view the future. We all have foresight, but we don't always make a habit of using it.

I remember when I was a new driver. I was driving down a long stretch of highway, and a buddy of mine was in the front seat. We were proceeding down the far-left side of a two-lane highway at night, and there was one car about three or four car lengths ahead of me. At that moment, I recalled my driver's ed training at Burlington Township High School. My wise trainer, Mr. Holden, spoke his first words once we started my driving lesson, and they were, *"Hey, slow down!"*

One of the skills I developed in driver's ed was the habit of glancing forward periodically to see what was going on several cars ahead of me. At the time, I could not imagine how important that skill would become.

Well, as my buddy and I were moving along at average speed, I could see about 50 or 60 yards ahead. I saw something that looked like an older-model white car "parked" in the same lane in which I was driving. As the car in front of me and I got closer, it became clear to me that it was definitely a car parked in the passing lane of a two-lane highway. But wait a minute. Something was wrong. The car in front of me wasn't slowing down! I pumped my brakes lightly with my eyes now fixed on both vehicles.

It all happened so fast, it seemed like a dream.

I thought the car would turn away at the last moment, but it didn't. WHAM! It smashed right into the rear of the parked car. I had just enough time to swerve into the right lane. The impact of the crash on the car directly in front of me was so severe, it spun towards me, and I almost crashed into it. I cut the wheels and quickly steered out of the way.

Through my rearview mirror, I saw that the driver was okay and that apparently, there was no one in the parked car. We could not believe what happened. It was incredible! That driver did not see the parked white car — the same one I noticed almost 70 yards back. How could that be? The answer is simple: The driver didn't see what was right in front of him because he wasn't paying attention. That is called a "distraction."

In life, even though you may have 20/20 vision and your foresight is free of dirt, cracks, chips, and frost, a momentary distraction could be deadly — to your dreams, that is.

Remember: We are making our way through the town of 'Adversity' and headed toward the city of 'Hope.' Two things are important here:

1. **Keep your windshield (your ability to look forward/foresight) clear; and**
2. **Be sure to carefully watch for distractions.**

In other words, while exercising foresight, make sure you have a clear vision of your future — of what is 60 or 70 yards ahead on the highway of life. As you look ahead, you will gain important knowledge.

While you are driving, it is so easy to get distracted and miss your turn. You could be talking with someone or just listening to your favorite song on the radio and miss a turn. After doing so, you must usually find a way to turn around. While getting back on the right track, you will lose time, energy, and valuable fuel.

## *Insight*

Let's talk about one of my favorites: insight. I will illustrate insight using the example of headlights. Insight means to quickly apprehend the true nature or inner character of something independent of a reasoning process. You might ask, *"What does that have to do with adversity and rebuilding hope?"* As we drive, there will be many things that aren't what they appear to be. There will also be things that are hard to understand exactly what they are.

Have you ever gone out right before sunrise when it's still dark outside? Everything is still and silent. There might be a couple of birds harmonizing, but that's it. Depending on whether or not you have left the porch light on or how far the streetlight is from your driveway, it can sometimes be a little spooky.

So, you attentively make your way to the car, climb inside, close the door, turn the key, and awaken your engine. When you turn on your headlights, you can suddenly see everything with crystal clear clarity. You observe insects, bits of paper on the ground, the neighbor's fence, and fumes floating past your window from your car's tailpipe. With those lights on, you can also see the imperfections in the windshield. You see so many things you didn't or couldn't see clearly just a moment ago—all because you turned on one simple switch: the headlights.

Turning on our insight may not be as easy as turning an on/off switch. Some people seem to be born with it, others find it through God, and many must simply work at it. One of the biggest hurdles in becoming more insightful is impulsiveness. We must learn to take quality time to think about our decisions. When we are young and immature, we often acted first and thought second. As adults, we must train ourselves to think first and act only after considering the repercussions.

Insight has several nicknames, including:

- **Intuition**
- **Gut feeling**
- **Sixth sense**
- **Discernment**

Remember, however, that insight operates independently of a reasoning process. In other words, it may not always make logical sense at first glance. Once you have insight into something, it will validate itself as it comes to fruition.

In overcoming adversity, insight will help you examine areas you may feel are unnecessary or uncomfortable. Understand this: Strong insight is not for the faint of heart. It will take courage to follow up on some of the things you find. In fact, as you progress, many of those insights will be all about YOU. When you are the kind of person who shows genuine interest in your own progression, you will be alright with insights that correct your words, attitudes, and actions. You will be a better person for it, too.

Insight is also important while advancing through adversity because it seems to give us comfort when we can piece together how the adversity originally occurred. We often receive quick bursts of information during adversity that will come from our hearts and not our heads, so expect them.

Lastly, let me append this topic to the idea of your insight headlights. Insight is not inerrant because it emanates from human nature. Everything is about us is subject to fallacy once in a while, so you will have episodes where you misread your insight. Don't be alarmed. Just keep moving forward.

Okay. We have cleaned our windshield, checked our rearview mirrors, and turned on our headlights. Now, fasten your seatbelt, and let's head for the open road.

Here we go!

## Chapter Two
## The Benefits of Adversity

Before I delve deeply into this next chapter, allow me to clarify something. When I say 'benefit,' this is what I mean:

A benefit is something that is advantageous or good. What I am conveying here is that some advantageous things can be discovered through adversity. Some might say I am an optimist. Well, okay. Yes, I am! However, the mindset I am describing is a little deeper than that.

Now, I am not diminishing the unfriendly nature of adversity. Rather, I am just suggesting that there are some valuables left behind after adversity has visited.

As you train your mind to identify and appreciate adversity's advantages, you can have more balance before, during, and after the experience. You must realize something good can be produced as you learn to view adversity from a new perspective. Where can you find a new perspective on adversity? I am glad you asked! You can find it right here in this book, of course!

I believe there are some clear benefits of adversity, to include:

- **Perseverance**
- **Focus**
- **Determination**
- **Poise**
- **Humility**

You may be asking, *"Can adversity really produce any of those positive characteristics?"* That's another excellent question!

Let's start with perseverance. First, let's define it. To persevere means "to continue in some effort, course of action, etc., despite opposition or difficulty."

Perseverance is an invaluable trait. As you launch out into any course of action, you will have plenty of opposition and difficulty. You will be faced with many quitting points. That's when it will look, feel, and sound like the ideal place to give up because you can't go on. Conversely, as you embrace perseverance, it will speak to you, saying, *"Don't give up. Keep going. Don't stop. Continue. Don't give up. Stick with it. Don't quit."* When you have a specific course of action that is positive, will develop you, and enrich others, it is critical that you persevere—not just for your benefit, but also for what it will mean to others.

Did you ever stop to think that your life's story might be the very thing that ignites ten other people to action? That kind of thinking should inspire us all to persevere. There is nothing that trains you on how to persevere like a string of adversities.

Let's discuss the sport of boxing for a moment. As beginners, some boxers are good fighters, but they have a "glass jaw" or "glass chin." Having a glass jaw means you can't take a solid punch without being shaken up or knocked down in boxing terminology.

As a young boy in elementary school, my older sister had a boyfriend named Lamont, whom she later married. He boarded his earth-to-Heaven commute in 2006 and is now in a much better place. Lamont taught me how to box. It seems like it was just yesterday, we were both standing downstairs in the family room of my mother's home in LaGorce Square. I must have been in the 4th or 5th grade at the time. I recall him saying, *"Keep your right hand up."* He showed me how to block a punch and how to jab.

Another important tactic Lamont taught me was the proper stance. A big part of how you respond after receiving a solid punch depends on your balance in boxing. Of course, maintaining balance requires having the proper stance. Your feet, although constantly moving, should be shoulder-width apart. One foot should be slightly forward, aligning your heel and toes together. A skilled fighter has mastered the proper stance. He can also take a good, strong, clean punch, shake it off, and continue.

Let me ask: Can you take a punch? How do you respond when life catches you with a clean shot to the "jaw"? It may have been rejection from an employment opportunity or promotion. Perhaps someone close to you suffered a health challenge and needed immediate hospitalization. Maybe a person you have cared about for years walked right out of your life. After the initial shock of the blow, what went through your mind? For most of us, many emotions run through our souls. However, after life delivered what was meant to be a knockout blow, you decided to persevere…to keep going.

After training with the sparring partner of adversity with that new attitude, you will learn to take a hit and continue to fight. You will gain the confidence that you can, indeed, persevere—and you will!

Another benefit of adversity is focus, as adversity can help you develop that ability. Focus means to fix or settle your eyes or mind on one thing; to concentrate. There is so much to accomplish in life but try to make up your mind to concentrate on one area at a time. If you intend to sharpen an area, you can move from one state of development to another in time.

You may be wondering how adversity can develop your focus. Again, we have defined adversity as misfortune, disaster, calamity, or trouble. Whenever trouble or misfortune comes around, it initially has our undivided attention. When adversity hits, most of us will begin to take stock. We examine ourselves to see if we are responsible for its cause. We concentrate on events, actions, words, or anything that may have been a factor in the situation. If we detect something was our fault, we will usually focus on trying not to make the same mistake again, all while rebuilding our lives with a renewed focus.

Adversity has used that technique to turn many weaknesses into strengths and can teach us to settle down our minds. It will also give us the courage needed to focus on specific areas of our lives. A new sense of focus can be a benefit of adversity. The ability to focus is invaluable. In fact, your focus can become the mark that helps someone else find their place.

I recall playing varsity sports in high school. What else? Football! I liked playing defense, although I loved playing fullback during my freshman year the most. The nose guard position was one I truly enjoyed. The nose guard (or nose tackle) is a position on the defensive line and is situated in the middle of the defensive line. His primary area of responsibility is to disrupt the offensive running game.

When I was in defensive formations, I was responsible for taking my position directly across from the football. I lined up in just a way to cover running plays that would come on either side of the ball. The other reason the coach had me do that was so the rest of the defense would know where the offensive players were lining up. Sometimes, they would set up in the center of the field. Other times, they would line up to the right or left side of the field. Occasionally, they would split the field; some on the right and some on the left. After each play was over, wherever the official would place the football was where I would be.

My position was critical to the defense because the rest of our defensive team would line up wherever I was, as I was always closest to the ball. I could not move until the center snapped the ball. No one could distract me — not the crowd, the quarterback, the other players, or even the cheerleaders. If I lost my focus, our team would have been penalized. Even during a timeout, I had to follow the ball. That took a lot of focus.

From 1980 to 1984, I had the honor of being a part of the Burlington Township High School Football Program. Overall, there is one memory that always stands out very vividly in my thoughts…

The game was an intense, hard-hitting, intelligent, jungle warfare kind of game. I remember the sun beaming a strong, steady heat onto the field. I can still recall the scent of medical spray and tape, which each player wore on both ankles to prevent sprains. Both teams had reached a critical moment in the cross-town rivalry.

At one point in the third quarter, I stood across from the ball while the other team took a timeout. Our defense had the other team pinned down on the five-yard line in their own territory. My muscles felt tense but were tuned like the strings of a handcrafted violin. My uniform was drenched in salty sweat, painted in strokes of vibrant green grass, splashes of deep red blood stains from cuts and scrapes, and a good portion was spotted with dark brown dirt and mud on my knees, elbows, and shoes.

During the timeout, my heart rate and breathing crept back down into the normal zone after revving at maximum

RPMs. Then, I loosened my helmet. My helmet was decorated with streaks of colors from other teams' helmets, a few gashes, and a proud falcon decal smeared beyond recognition. With helmet in hand, I took a knee. A young man with emergency room urgency ran onto the field and handed me a bottle of water.

Our gritty, in-your-face coaches had trained us never to allow our attention to roam all over the stadium. *"Stay focused,"* they said. I quickly took a risky glance toward a spot by the fence near the goalpost just to check one more time. *"Yes!"* I screamed inside with my usual coolness. *"There he is!"*

Ladies and gentlemen, it was my dad! Our eyes locked briefly, and my chest felt as if it grew two inches. There he stood, with his newspaper folded and tucked neatly under his arm and reading glasses in one hand. He couldn't make many of my games because he was busy operating and managing his own successful business, and I understood that. I believed the look he gave me said, *"I'm proud of you, son. You are keeping a sports family tradition alive. Now, shut them down!"* I honestly cannot recall whether we won that day, but I remember my dad being there. Over the years, I have also thought about my teammates and how we learned to focus and win together.

Remember: When a new demand to focus arises in you, embrace it. It just may be the one thing that holds a team together. You may have the ability to focus on one area, whereas someone else may not be able to focus well in the same area. However, there may be a team of champions that needs your concentration—your focus.

Another offshoot of adversity can be determination. Determination means to be resolute or to have or show a fixed purpose. It means to be unwavering.

Many of us have a competitive side. When we play, work, or are a part of something, we want to win or at least do our very best. Sometimes when going through adversities, calamities, or disasters, we get the sinking feeling that we are losing the battle. When going through a difficult experience, we can tell when we are letting it affect us more than we should. Our edge might be slipping, our focus bouncing around, and perseverance is losing altitude, causing us to feel like giving up. It's at that point when we must decide.

We resolve to do whatever we must to make it through the adverse situation. We set the dial of our minds to "forward." We will have to have a strong determination to make it through some adversities, or we never will. We can find a new level of determination when we are faced with adversity.

Yes, it is true. Determination can be produced from adversity. Here's how:

When disaster and calamity strike, they challenge your hope and desire to obtain a dream. When adversity shows up, it never checks with you to see whether it is a good time or not. Sometimes, it opens your door, right when it seems like you are getting ready to accomplish a goal, dream, or vision. It may strike in your last year of college. It may occur just as you have scratched and clawed your way out of debt.

I have had friends and loved ones hospitalized for months, then they undergo some form of treatment, and it looks as if their situation is turning around. Just when they begin to feel relief, things suddenly take a turn for the worse — sometimes, much worse.

Often, when you seem like you are right in the middle of change, things collapse. It's at that point when you should take a look at the dream you were just about to conquer. Your conscience may debate with you, asking, *"Is this selfish to continue this pursuit?"* It bargains, argues, and reasons with you, even suggesting it would be irrational to keep moving forward. Initially, you might resist, but all too often, resistance wears you down. It is difficult in life to pick up your hope or dream and run with it again after you have set it down for a minute or two.

Adversity and destiny wrestle like two young brothers over a new jacket given by mom that fits them both. Occasionally, they fight to the bitter end. As you allow your hope to spring back again and again, you will be left with a more profound sense of determination. It's strange because once you have determination, you feel like you can get more.

Once you stayed determination to reach one goal, don't you feel as if you can reach the next one and the next? It's awesome!

Now, watch out because soon, you will have focus and determination working together. You will fix and settle your mind on something and concentrate and, while you do, you will have determination and resolve. You will be fixed, set, and unwavering. Those two characteristics (focus and determination) are sometimes inborn, but they can also be sharpened through adversity.

There's another side of the word 'benefit.'

For example, when you start a new job, you are typically excited about the benefits package, the salary, or both. Healthcare, dental, retirement, stock options, and all other kinds of perks can come as benefits of a particular job—but you must first qualify for them. You must complete a certain amount of time, have good attendance, and strong performance. Qualification is not automatic.

When calamity, disaster, and trouble come your way, you have a choice. Don't let adversity run over you. It's all about how you choose to respond. You can decide to be bitter, resentful, and separate yourself in your personal solitary confinement. You can opt to camouflage your reality with something toxic like prescription drug abuse and alcohol. You can also stay positive and move forward, leading the way to reap the benefits of adversity.

As you progress through this book, you will gain a better understanding of the benefits shared within and many that are not once you obtain the know-how of Overcoming the Storms of Adversity.

The next benefit of adversity is poise. Poise means to be balanced. It means to have composure and is the condition of being calm. After going through several misfortunes, you will learn some things. Many of us are familiar with panic. The more paralyzed with fear we become, the worse things seem. Panic throws us out of orbit and makes focusing almost impossible.

When I am stressed out, my ability to focus is altered. Consequently, I can make a tough situation worse by making an unwise decision amid adversity. My negative emotions can sometimes have a ripple effect. Other people catch my anger, resentment, or fear like a common cold.

One of the best but not always the easiest ways to advance through adversity is to have poise. Practice makes perfect! With enough of it, you can learn to remain calm in adversity. When you remain calm, you can think and articulate better. Adversity can teach you to be calm amid turmoil, usually after you have learned from its consequences. Poise is what we all need during adversity.

When I think of the poise, I envision a young model who is just learning how to walk the runway. I can almost hear the stern words of her modeling coach: *"Poise! Poise! You must have poise!"* I imagine a young, gifted, sleekly framed model with flawless skin, and angel white smile, and finely sculpted hair with each strand set in perfect harmony. Gracefully, she alternates her arms' sway with legs and feet moving while her shoulders are back, and her chin is leveled. That beautiful image would not be complete without the book perched atop her head as she walks. That illustration of poise reflects someone moving from one place to another with balance, composure, and grace.

When adversity comes, keep walking toward your destiny and hope. But, while you are doing it, keep your balance and don't lose your composure. Stay calm and keep it steady. While you are walking, keep your mind calm and balanced. Balance your thoughts. Don't get too high with your highs, and don't get too low with your lows. Sooner or later, your poise will become natural, and you can rest the book back on the shelf.

The last benefit of adversity I'm going to discuss is humility. Humility is having or showing a consciousness of one's defects or shortcomings. How conscious are we of our shortcomings? Do we even believe we have them?

Have you ever met a person who refuses to accept responsibility for their negative actions? It's annoying, right?

I often look at my own life and ask myself, *"Where would I be without trouble?"* Would I be a proud person if the adversity in my life had not humbled me? Would I be able to walk past the person at the fast-food restaurant who's panhandling and not understand the shame and embarrassment they feel? Without misfortune, would I be able to sit across from a young man who's sobbingly resting his head in both hands because he feels as if the negative things in his life will never change? Without trouble and disaster, would I be listening closely to the 30-something couple as they tried desperately to piece their financial picture together after being overwhelmed with regret for not having pursued their dreams earlier?

The answer to those questions is no.

Without adversity in my life, I would not be able to identify and connect with others who have had similar experiences. I would be a very "proud" person if adversity did not humble me.

As a young high school athlete, I was arrogant. I think that as an adult, I would have been worse without adversity. In my line of work, as I help people, it is an added feature of adversity. In counseling, people feel at ease because they can detect genuine understanding as they open the safe deposit box of their deepest and most painful experiences.

But let's get back to humility.

One thing about adversity is that it usually exposes our weaknesses. Most are aware of our own shortcomings to some degree or another, but it is a whole different ballgame when others are made equally aware. When that happens, there is no covering…nothing to hide behind. That is humility in its purest form.

I believe if humility didn't happen, we would act in front of others as if we didn't have shortcomings. Unfortunately, when some people find out about our shortcomings, they will never forget.

You might still be asking, *"How can humility benefit me?"* Well, adversity that causes humility is like insurance. It is a guarantee that can help us maintain an honest estimation of ourselves most of the time. We will know where we are—and where we aren't. Adversity does not discriminate. It will touch us all.

# Chapter Three
# Breakdown or Breakthrough?

Why do some people break down during adversity while others don't? We see it happen around us all the time. Male and female. Young and old. So many people face adversity with a vast array of responses.

What I am offering you here is simply a few keys on how to have a breakthrough and not a breakdown during adversity.

So, what do I mean by "breakthrough"? The word itself has several differing meanings, but there's one that best explains it as we discuss breaking through adversity: A sudden development that removes a barrier to progress. That is what we must learn to do while going through adversity—and even when we are not. We must remove the barriers that obstruct the pathway to growth in our lives. I'm aware doing so may be a new attitude for some but know we can all benefit from a new way of thinking every now and then. To grow and develop in life, you must be willing to face and embrace new concepts. More of the same will, indeed, produce more of the same! The concept of learning to find something valuable in negative circumstances will not be easy, but I believe you are up for the challenge. I've read many writings on the subject and agree with most of them.

However, there's something I want to add to the idea: self-image—how you see yourself. There are two parts to how you see yourself. The first one is critical, as it involves how you see yourself in the mirror. How do you feel about your eyes, nose, hairline, and physique? Do you accept yourself as you are right now? Be careful with comparing yourself to others. Learn to love yourself. There's probably something in all of us we would change here or there if we could.

You, my friend, are a masterpiece and intelligently designed. Celebrate your uniqueness! When you view yourself in the mirror, accept what you see and be glad it's different from everyone else. There's only one "you"—unless you are one of multiple births (i.e., twins, triplets, etc.). Even then, there is something about you that will be exclusively "you."

It's story time!

Years ago, I was a counselor at a recovery center. I remember a particular young lady at the facility who would constantly state she was ugly. I didn't think much of it until I realized she wasn't just joking around. I observed she was very consistent in her declaration and that her demeanor was very serious. I recall asking her, *"What do you see when you look in the mirror?"*

*"I see a very ugly person,"* came her reply.

Later, in a meeting held with other counselors at the facility, information surfaced that the young lady was abused as a child. The strange thing was no one shared the young lady's opinion. She was not at all unattractive! Still, what everyone else could see was not what she saw when she looked in the mirror. She could not change the picture of the ugly thing that happened to her as a child.

I think many experiences in life paint across an internal canvas with soft brushes, which, in turn, form self-image. Some people have within the ability to see themselves moving forward, no matter what. One reason is because of that inner painting. It is as if they are unstoppable! They can almost see themselves having a positive response in a disastrous situation before it happens. When adversity or misfortune occurs, they already have a BluRay DVD playing of themselves advancing., allowing themselves to break through adversity instead of breaking down under it.

On the other hand, other people seem to have just the opposite experience. They can almost always imagine the worst and see themselves breaking down under pressure no matter the situation.

I believe we all have an inner portrait. You may say, *"I don't feel or see any self-image or self-portrait."* You may not believe any of this is true, and that's okay. If that is you, give this a try: Consistently behave in a way that is contrary to how you presently perceive yourself.

Have you ever observed an individual from an urban area relocate to the country? How about a person who excels in academia suddenly trying to acclimate to a hip-hop scene? Consider the proud senior who has worked honorably for 30 or 40 years and then retires. Each scenario can be challenging, as it forces that individual to jump right into something that is the opposite of what they've done for a long time. One reason is that they were comfortable and settled doing what they have "always done." Another reason change is not easy is that they have seen themselves on that inner canvas performing the tasks repeatedly. It became a part of the masterpiece produced — their inner self-portrait.

I think that just about every day, something is being added or subtracted from our self-portrait. A new color here. A brushstroke there. There's always a new line drawn somewhere. Self-image is a remarkable feature that humans possess. By itself, it is neutral. It must be influenced by some other force and will accept whatever it is consistently given.

As we discuss the concept of the inner portrait, consistency is key. In order to grasp self-image, you must understand that reality. It is what we consistently accept about ourselves that will stick to the canvas. It's what we hear, see, or think over and over…and over. That is one way our inner portrait is painted, which is why I am an avid supporter of positive affirmations, especially when they involve young people.

Recently, I was in a supermarket when my heart sank. Walking at a medium pace and pushing a shopping cart that limped down the aisle with one wheel protesting the trip was a mother and two darling children. The youngest child sat in his imaginary cockpit. His two chubby legs protruded from the designated openings in the shopping cart's frame. He wore fitted white socks on his little feet, sporting those all-American standard baby shoes. Suddenly, the other child darted to the other side of the aisle with gazelle-like speed and agility and knocked over one of the displays. Intuitively, the mother realized the young child had secretly drifted behind her but was picked up on her radar. She turned around just before he could collide with the parallel parked display. *"Get over here! You are so stupid!"* she said with obvious disdain for the child's antics. At that moment, sorrow surged like waters of high tide at sunset from deep in my soul.

The problem with those seed-like words, thoughts, and actions is that by the time we grow old enough to understand their meanings, we're probably already sculpted by them. Far too often, those negative experiences assist in breaking down instead of breaking through. I'll use myself as an example.

As early as I can remember, I was fed a healthy diet of positive affirmations from a loving Christian family environment and business. Positive words, imagery, examples, and training were all painted on my inner canvas. However, somewhere in my teen years, it was as if an unfamiliar hand joined in on my canvas' design. There suddenly appeared a different style, striking new colors, and varying brush strokes.

What we must learn to do is take an active role in painting our self-portraits. What is it that we really think, say, and envision about ourselves? It is never too late and surely never too early to take that brush in our own hands and paint. Our actions tend to align themselves with our inner portrait, even if it is not a good one or was painted by someone else.

Take a minute to do some self-reflecting. What do you see? Do you look intelligent, healthy, and wealthy? Or do you look sad, insecure, and just out of it? You might ask, *"Why should I think any of those things are important?"* It is because your mind and soul are like an engine. Your physique is like the chassis of an automobile. You can only perform in accordance with your engine. A motorcycle will always accelerate differently from a sports utility vehicle. Likewise, a compact economy car will never handle the road like an expensive, intelligent, high-performance, hypnotic, cat-like automobile. So, who we really are is based on what type of engine, CPU, or attitude lies beneath our hoods.

If you feel you are suffering because of a poor self-image, here's what you can do to change it:

First, never again accept negative thoughts, words, or images about yourself from others. Take that negative paintbrush out of their hands. Some people will stand just to pull you down. It's as if they like to see if they can push your buttons. Don't let them! Take the initiative by not giving those people that much power over your destiny. If you let them take advantage of you, they will. Never let another person's opinion of you define you. Far too many people today are locked up under the confinement of someone else's opinion or perception of them. That is dangerous! You don't want to live your life being someone other than who you were designed to be just because someone thought you should.

The second thing you can do to change a poor self-image is never again accepting negative thoughts, words, or images about yourself from you. Often, we can be our own worst critics. We can be ruthless in pursuit of our own defects. We must learn to sometimes cut ourselves a break. It's good to set healthy goals, dreams, and aspirations, but what happens when we fall short? Do our failures define us? They shouldn't. Just because we fail, that does not make us failures. In fact, failure can be turned into success if we learn from it. I believe we must sometimes fail in order to reach success, but many of us have had life brand us as a failure just because we failed a few times.

The same "me" who occasionally insists I am one of the greatest human beings will flip-flop and list reasons why I am one of the worst. Think about this: Would you let others treat you the way you sometimes treat yourself?

There are times when things don't turn out the way you planned. The best thing you can do is sit back and analyze that outcome. Find out where you went wrong, and fix it. We all need to do that in order to be better. We can't stay in "that place." We must move on.

The reality is sometimes, other people say negative things about us, just as we say negative things about ourselves. When that happens, what should we do? Whether it is in school, on the job, or at home, how do we respond when we feel others trying to plant negative seeds in us? We must resist and fight back! We can't be passive or neutral here. The battle is not always external, though. There are times when the only way we can resist negativity will be from the inside.

You must know who you are and remind yourself by watering your own crops every once in a while. You should not just accept what is being said to you, especially when it is negative. Even if it comes from within you, you must learn to resist and fight against it. Sometimes, it will seem like an all-out war. Why? Because some of the people who have something negative to say to you will be the same ones you love and respect the most. They will be the ones who can profoundly influence you. Those things they say and do can go very deep. Nonetheless, resist in a loving, respectful, and, if necessary, forceful way. Never accept negativity's presence being painted on your canvas.

The last thing you can do if you are suffering from a poor self-image is this: Plant a fresh crop of positive thoughts, words, and images in your own soul. Take the brush in your own hand and go to work. How, you ask? Talk, think, and learn to imagine good things about yourself. Sometimes, people who observe you doing just that will think you are arrogant, but there is a significant difference in what I am suggesting to you here.

Modesty says, *"I am as good as anyone else."*

Arrogance says, *"I am better than everyone else."*

There is nothing wrong with self-confidence, but people lose touch with reality when they think they are absolutely — beyond question — better than everybody. Some of us are better at one thing, while others are better at something else. Conversely, some people are good at many things. When we are honest with ourselves, we will learn there are things in which we are also deficient. We should always try to strengthen our weaknesses.

## Chapter Four
## P.O.W. (Prisoner of War)

Before I begin this chapter, I want to preface it by saying this: The decision to include this content as a part of this work was difficult. The reason I faced difficulties was because of my love and concern for my family and loved ones.

**********

When soldiers go off to war, they carry a small piece of each family member's heart with them. When I decided to enlist in "the war," I became a prisoner. I suffered deep, self-inflicted wounds and chronic emotional pain. However, gone are the years of constant anguish over consistent, unwise decisions and their rippling ramifications. Healed are the wounds of heart and soul caused by the neglect of healthy relationships and the quality time that accompanied them. Almost unnoticeable are the scars I carry due to causing so much shame, anxiety, and heartache.

I have a friend who injured a knee many years ago in a car accident. *"Eventually, it healed almost perfectly,"* he conveyed. *"It feels just as strong and is just as flexible as it did before the accident."* Decades later, every once in a while, a simple thing like moisture from a soaking rain caused him to flinch with a spastic twinge.

It is said that time heals all wounds, but does it? Does time heal those who've been deeply wounded? Does time heal the wounds that some receive from wounding others? Can time heal the wounds that loved ones received by being repeatedly wounded by those they love?

Perhaps.

That response is not self-pity, self-condemnation, or depression. It is simply the reconstituted heart of a very fortunate man attempting to articulate reality. Much has been regained, and even more have been added to my life, for which I am grateful to God. Yet, there are a few irreplaceable spoils I relinquished in "the war" of drug addiction—"me vs. me"—that can never be recaptured. Time, closeness, and rare opportunities are several of those treasures.

**********

Yes! I did it! Cap and gown, achievements, proud parents, applause… I was a graduate of the Class of 1984 from Burlington Township High!

Several of my friends had spoken with an Army recruiter. I watched their enthusiasm, excitement, and, of course, their own unique brand of patriotism. They were convinced the military would be a great opportunity for them, and they were right. Internally, I admired them for the decisions they made. They even tried time and again to persuade me. They even convinced the recruiter to visit my home to speak with me. At the time, I thought, *"Wow! My friends think an awful lot of me!"* (I don't know if it was that **OR** they just wanted to have someone to hang out with in case they were shipped out or stationed overseas.) In the early 80s, there were no threats of war, but somewhere in the back of my mind, I couldn't help but wonder what would happen if a real war were to occur. What if one of my buddies got wounded or was captured?

Anyway, I didn't think I had enough self-discipline to deal with the Army. Maybe I sold myself short. Maybe not. I felt some of the stories about those basic training drill sergeants were intimidating, but most of my friends stuck with it and are better men and women because of it.

Somewhere around my early 20s, I found myself in a war against the armed forces of addiction — something I battled for several years. My command post was the church. My mind became the battlefield. The only way I could win the war was with the help of God Almighty.

For many years, I conducted reconnaissance on that enemy. I studied him well, only to be targeted and hit time and again by hostile fire. I had altercations with the law...and several brushes with death. I took some basic training at AA (Alcoholics Anonymous), NA (Narcotics Anonymous), and several rehabs. At times, I thought I had lost the war and would remain captured and imprisoned by the enemy of drugs and alcohol forever. In my eyes, I had become a P.O.W. — a Prisoner of War.

I realize you might say, *"That really doesn't compare to a real war like in Afghanistan or Iraq."* You're correct, but there are some similarities.

The most significant difference was that my addiction became a war against me that I decided to enlist in and re-enlist. Conversely, combat is usually not something we choose to start because no one likes war's harsh realities.

Death.

Post-Traumatic Stress Disorder.

Dismemberment.

Family displacement.

Those are just a few of the painful experiences associated with war.

If adversity is misfortune, calamity, trouble, and disaster, addiction is one of the presidential suites at "The Grand Aversity Hotel."

Right now, you might be thinking, *"That information is very personal. Why be so transparent, Rodney?"* That is a very, very good question. I considered it for a while before I began writing this book several years ago. I asked myself, *"Do I really want to be this open about my life? Some people have never known this side of me – at least not in this much detail."* Even now, I sometimes catch myself deliberating over the reality of sharing so much about my personal life.

Suddenly, I was enveloped in a massive cloud of purpose. I quickly remembered one of the main reasons I was willing to share some of my past experiences: It's for **OTHER** people. If it is possible to dissuade one individual from going down the wrong road, telling my story is worth it.

"That road" was one that started for me in the 1980s. It was paved with the fresh asphalt and newly-painted yellow lines of popularity, the prestigious underworld of entrepreneurial circles, and modest materialism. That smooth road slowly and methodically peeled and flaked away until it became a narrow, dark, dirt-laden country road. On it was my broken dreams, broken people, broken glass, broken promises, and seemingly unbreakable shackles around the minds of those of us who traveled it.

There is another reason I am not uneasy disclosing details about my past. Once you take an old white rag and dip it in deep burgundy dye, it will never be as it was before. You may lessen the stain, but it will never be the same white rag. I can be transparent today because I am discussing who I was, not who I am. I am extremely confident in who I have become. In fact, that is who I was always supposed to be. So, in celebration of who I have become, along with empowering others, those are two reasons I am willing to tell my story.

Now, let's go deeper.

I remember getting siphoned into the underworld of cocaine use by a friend. It all seemed cool, casual, and fun. In a very short period of time, the drug had coiled itself around my soul like a boa constrictor and was squeezing the life right out of me.

My self-respect. Squeezed.

My dreams. Squeezed.

The dignity of my family's name. Squeezed.

My health. Squeezed.

And, of course, my money. Squeezed.

I have learned something about war along the way, though. A good soldier is a bad choice for the enemy to capture because he will never accept being captured no matter what. He will never stop planning his escape. He will never stop thinking about how to destroy the device that is holding him. His mind doesn't sleep, his body doesn't seem to tire, and he will never surrender. Eventually, he will become more trouble to his captors than they believe he is worth. It's even likely he will wound or kill one or more of his enemies while trying to escape, unless he is killed first. Daily, he thinks to himself, "Today, I will be free."

I don't consider myself a war hero, but I am a decorated enlisted officer in the war against addiction. Yet, as I departed for war, I did not go alone. Let me shade in an idea I sketched out for you earlier: time and wounds.

On my self-inflicted tour of duty, I took with me a proud father, Hollie—a second-generation African American entrepreneur who produced one male offspring. I was the child whom he thought would one day help hold the reigns of ownership in the family business—one he had built himself.

Also emotionally attached to me was my incurably optimistic, faith-filled mother, Constance Naomi—a woman who, many years ago, gave birth to this 10-pound, pale-skinned, curly brown-haired baby boy. Prior to conception, she prayed earnestly for a male child who God Himself would one day use. She experienced heartache and heartbreak after being informed her son had been captured by "the enemy." My mother is known for her bravery, as for weeks, she would turn on the nightly news expecting to hear the report that her son was no longer alive.

In addition to my parents were my two sisters, Donna and Kim. They, too, were getting hit by the shrapnel of my life as it exploded like an old shell. They are two young women who cared about and respected me. One of them is older than I. The other is younger. They expected me to go on to college and maybe even some kind of professional sports career, only to have their expectations of their brother shattered like glass on a concrete walkway. Nevertheless, my sisters had a keen ability to always—and I do mean always—encourage me. When I needed it the most, they seemed to be able to reach beyond their own pain and find a way to help push me further. I loved and needed them, just as I still do now.

I still experience tiny shards of regret from actions that occurred all those years ago. I have apologized enough, been depressed enough, relived negative decisions, and paid various costs. Today, my family and friends, as well as the Creator, let me know I am deeply loved, forgiven, and accepted.

Again, when I mention war, don't think I take it lightly or misunderstand its brutality. I have a niece who recently returned from military deployment in Afghanistan after 18 months. Every day, we prayed—just as she did—for protection and a safe return. I am proud of her. In fact, both of my nieces were very respectful and kind during my years as a prisoner. I love you both, Carlesha and Chanel, and my nephew, Tamon.

I am also grateful for a small battalion of Navy Seal-type Christians led by my mother, who would not stop praying for me: The International Crusade Choir, "The Crusaders," who did so much more than sing. Their prayers made me like one of those P.O.W.s that wouldn't die and couldn't be killed. Somehow, someway, no matter how bad things got, I could not completely abandon hope. Although I tried, I could never lay back and recline in the idea of becoming a career addict.

Still, I felt like a P.O.W. My will was shackled. I had no control over my decision-making. So many times, I knew the consequences of my actions could be severe, but I felt totally unable to veer away from them.

There are countless stories I could tell of episodes during my addiction, I could probably write a book. However, I will share one here. As the curtain draws, there is no glitter, glamour, or glory. I'm sharing just the facts.

Nearly two decades ago, far removed from the LaGorce Square suburbs of Burlington Township, where I grew up, I lived and worked in a hardcore drug house during the height of my addiction. The "employee package" consisted of room, board, and a salary. Meals were usually miniscule. At the time, my salary was $100 to $200 a day that was dispersed in the underworld currency of cocaine or crack cocaine paid hourly. Cash was in NO way an option. There was also limited alcohol and whatever other drugs I could mooch or skim from our "clients" (as we referred to them). Clients were people who would pay to come into the house and use drugs.

I was known only as "Rock." The staff consisted of the "Manager" (known as the houseman or lady), their partner, one or two female hostesses, a girl (prostitute), a runner (a person to go and make runs to get drugs), a trapper (usually an in-house drug dealer), one or two lookouts (to keep an eye out for the authorities or other outside threats approaching), and the boss who lived offsite and could usually be contacted by one person through telephone code (we used pagers back then). The boss had one "job": drop and collect. Occasionally, he would threaten, torture, or shoot someone to protect his assets.

Let's not lose sight of the theme I am talking about here: **PRISONERS OF WAR.** From the lookouts to the bosses, we were all psychologically and spiritually incarcerated. That was my belief, anyway…

I recall one particular evening, all was quiet at the renowned southside home-based business, commonly referred to as a "crack house."

*SIDEBAR: Don't ever refer to a crack house as a crack house while in a crack house.*

It was a Saturday night. Suddenly, there was a knock at the door. The sound thundered and shook the entire first floor.

**BOOM! BOOM! BOOM!**

On the other side stood two women, probably in their late twenties. One was Black; the other was White. Actually, before we saw them, we heard them. One of them said, *"Open the door 'cause we got money!"* When the door was opened, we noticed that one woman had her arm around the other's neck and was kind of holding her up. As they entered, we could plainly see one of them had been shot. A trail of blood ran down her left leg. In her hand, she held several crumpled $20.00 bills stained with blood.

*"I can't believe this! This is crazy!"* I thought.

The women had already been "shopping," meaning they had already purchased drugs on the outside. They did so to bypass all the hidden fees drug house establishments added, such as purchasing drugs, renting drug paraphernalia, providing matches, or extending time. There was also a fee if help was needed with preparing the drugs, and yet another fee if the "visitor" suffered a drug-induced paranoia that was commonly known as skitzin', geekin', or tweetin'.

How about a quick biology refresher?

In the brain, there is a neurotransmitter called dopamine. Dopamine travels across gaps in the nerve cells called synapses. When we engage in something pleasurable, dopamine is released. It normally reabsorbs back into the bloodstream after giving us that feel-good sensation. When cocaine or its hybrid-derivative (crack cocaine) is absorbed into the bloodstream, several things occur. One thing that happens is the reabsorption process is interrupted. That overloads the central nervous system with dopamine, causing a sense of prolonged euphoria, heightened senses, and extreme paranoia—referred to as skitzin.

Moving along.

As the staff argued about accepting the two clients, the women hobbled over to the kitchen table and started using their drugs. Someone asked them, *"Don't you think you should go to the hospital first?"* They both replied, *"No. Everything is cool."* After quickly ingesting their first batch of drugs, reality set in. The Black girl said to her friend, *"Girl, you've been shot! You gotta get to the hospital!"* They immediately paid their fees and scurried out the door, leaving a trail of blood behind.

Their sudden jolt of reality was contagious. Suddenly, a torrent of intelligent thoughts and deep emotions rushed through my mind:

*"Man, this is like some crazy movie or something…but it ain't!"*

*"Yo, what am I doing up in here?!"*

*"Did I just work and hustle like crazy to win a job working in a crack house, even though they keep telling me it isn't one?"*

*"Yo, everybody here has trained themselves not to feel. They only care about one thing. I still feel!"*

*"Those two chicks that just came in…we should have called 911 from the beginning."*

*"We knew it was wrong, but we did it anyway, just for drugs and money."*

*"What if she would have died because the bullet was still traveling through her body? What if they both had kids?"*

*"What if whoever shot her is outside getting ready to finish the job and spray the whole house with bullets?"*

"I can't take this. I feel sick. Plus, I can't seem to stay high enough, man!"

"Every time my high goes down, my pain comes up!"

"I still hurt!"

"I miss my family, I lost a good job…again, and I know my mom is stressing. I love her."

"Oh, yeah. Where am I going to look next in this house to find a place where the mice aren't so friendly, and hands don't tip-toe through my pockets while I sleep?"

"I wish they would have shot me."

"I gotta get out of here…"

"Word. As soon as I finish mopping up this blood, I'm out!"

Then, I heard a female coworker call out, *"Hey, Rock! You look like you trippin' over there. You alright?"*

A dial in my mind turns two places to the right. Click, click! *"Yeah. It's all good."* And just like that, I'm back in the grip of addiction's hold.

Although the story is heart-wrenching and sad, there are many others like it and, unfortunately, are not uncommon in many inner cities of America. My story was used to display a small snapshot of the underworld prison camp called drug addiction.

I am extremely fortunate. Today, many of those who were in that "prison" with me are still hopeless, incarcerated, suffering from mental decline, or deceased. That is not to say I am alone. That is far from the truth. Thousands of men and women have used many different vehicles to escape the prison camp of drug addiction. Many of them have gone on to be productive in life.

In fact, I would like to take this time to express my deep appreciation for two organizations that were instrumental in my personal journey to freedom: Mission Teens and Victory Outreach International. Notice I used the word "freedom." Freedom is a powerful word. I am communicating the word in the same context in which it most commonly pops into our minds, much like liberty as opposed to slavery or bondage, and action without restraints.

I have migrated from sobriety, to recovery, to personal freedom, but I could not have accomplished it alone. There are thousands of programs that offer sobriety. There are a lot fewer that offer freedom. I would like to thank Mission Teens Bible Training Centers. That spiritual movement, which is headquartered in Norma, New Jersey, has organizations around the country. The centers have built into their structures an order by which time and spiritual growth qualify their clientele for increased liberties, responsibilities, and opportunities to be a part of the staff. After graduating from their residential program in 2001, I stayed on as a counselor and eventually, an Overseer. I learned accountability, service, and leading by example. Special thanks are given to Rev. Jim Bracken, Founder, and Tim Simmonds, Executive Director.

In 1997, I entered Victory Outreach International's Men's Recovery Home of North Philadelphia. Victory Outreach is a global movement spanning 33 countries. It is the largest of its kind in the world. Seven out of ten people who enter their Christian recovery homes are permanently changed. I learned countless spiritual realities and principles from Victory Outreach's North Philadelphia and Washington, DC branches.

I graduated from the men's home in 10 ½ months (with honors). Eventually, I made it through the reentry phase of the program. Finally, I had the high honor of being selected to serve in leadership in the Victory Outreach Church in Washington, DC. The organization has given me a dominant thread that has woven itself through the tapestry of my life: **VISION**.

I wish to extend heartfelt thanks to Victory Outreach International, its Elders, Pastors, Home Directors, Lay Leaders, recovery homes, and congregation. Great appreciation and respect go to Regional Pastor Titus Buelna, Pastor Ephrain Diaz, Pastor Joseph Bishop, Pastor/Evangelist Chuck Turner, Sr., and, of course, its Founders, Elder/Pastors Sonny and Julie Arguinzoni, Sr. Thank you for believing in me, loving me, and entrusting me with treasure.

Not many days go by that I don't remember the faces and the places involved in my struggle. Sometimes, no matter how hard I fight, negative memories slip past the gates and into my mind like a terrorist with plans to kill. When I experience those negative memories, I cultivate two attitudes.

The first thought is gratitude. I can't begin to articulate the kind of gratitude I now possess. I am grateful to behold the warm smile and dancing eyes of a warrior mom. I am grateful I will never have to be awakened by another sunrise tapping at the window of the abandoned car I slept in. I am grateful I will never again feel the piercing stares and brisk strides of a mother as she passes by the corner store with her child inside. I am grateful I will never pay another bridge toll on my way to do something self-destructive while screaming, *"I don't want to do this,"* as my soul switches to auto-pilot, and I keep driving. I am also grateful I will never have to solve the mathematical equation of how I spent a couple of thousand dollars in three days with nothing to show for it. I am grateful I will never have another encounter with the salty savor of tears cascading down an unshaven face as I pass by a lively church congregation where they are singing, clapping, and dancing to a freedom once known.

Wow. I remember that day so clearly. I paused but kept on walking. That beautiful choir's harmony was soon overpowered by the sound of painful, thick, iron shackles chained to my soul—a sound very familiar to a P.O.W.

I'm grateful. I am so appreciative that there was a God who not only loved me at my worst but also threw me a life preserver.

Secondly, after carefully considering those thoughts, I shifted gears to some of the people I knew back then. I daydreamed about the opportunity to run into them somewhere. Occasionally, I do and can share with them some incredibly good news.

Now, if you are reading this and still going through any phase of sobriety, recovery, or freedom, I want to encourage you. First, let me say I am not just talking about drug and alcohol abuse. There are many vehicles and various avenues to the destination called "out of control." Whatever it is that may be your personal battleground, let me say this: As long as you are alive, there is a chance you can win. There is hope. There is a literal light right at the edge of that dark passageway. Here's the thing, though: You must fight. I want to let you know (from experience) that the fight will be tough. Your opponent will not die easily. He will be very effective in his struggle against you. Why? Because he has been trained by one of the best—**YOU**! It will take an extreme brand of determination to be victorious.

I know someone is reading this section out of desperation and necessity. Maybe you are reading this on your own or as a recommendation from someone who cares. Either way, I am glad you are here.

All who have been captured by the enemy of addiction and escaped have achieved a major accomplishment. It takes more courage and determination than you could ever imagine to even dream of an escape for some people. Many do it every day, but you may never read about them. In war, there is always a painful reminder of fallen comrades. I remember several. In wars, there are many casualties. Some have been injured. Many others have seen combat seemingly unscathed but leave the battlefield suffering chronically from Post-Traumatic Stress Disorder. Some return home in one piece but never return psychologically.

I have seen many unfortunate scenarios involving addiction during my life. They have played out right before my eyes in alleys, parked cars, and abandoned buildings of the inner cities. I am not proud of that slice of the American pie, yet I am extremely fortunate that by God's grace, I have escaped the war and its aftermath—physically, spiritually, emotionally, and even socially. Still, there is a story to be told.

There are many out there who are still waging a losing war. They wake up every morning to deploy in another battle between themselves and addiction. To those, I say: You **CAN** overcome that adversity, but it will take every ounce of desire and determination you have to really be set free, along with the help of a close, personal friend of mine—Jesus Christ!

# Chapter Five
# How to Win Against Adversity

It's been established that adversity can be misfortune, calamity, trouble, or disaster. Before we delve in on how to win against it, let's talk about what it means to win.

When you mention the words "the winner," all kinds of thoughts arrive at the scene. Feelings of being a champion. A heart that palpitates as an enormous crowd dazzles the air with music performed by hands in a symphony of applause. Maybe you envision a mosaic parade in the air. You see a kaleidoscope of prancing ticker-tape coasting towards the earth. Perhaps the taste of deep satisfaction that comes from contributing to a team effort is what winning means to you. It doesn't always have to be a team or even sports, for that matter. It could be a special project from work that you completed ahead of time. It could be defeating a debilitating habit. Occasionally, it's the sensation of beating that obnoxious driver to that prime supermarket space while they tried to outmaneuver you. *"Yes! I beat you!"* screams your thoughts, all while concealing the celebration with an innocent grin. All of those examples and many more connect us to the experience of winning.

There is, however, one special group that seems to consistently defy the odds when it comes to winning against adversity: cats. One of the greatest forms of misfortune for a cat is to experience a fall or to be dropped unexpectedly. We are all very familiar with the adage that says, *"Cats always land on their feet."* It turns out that the aphorism is true (for the most part), but why is that? How do cats consistently win against the misfortune of falling, being dropped, or thrown? Humans sure don't exhibit that remarkable trait!

Much like humans, cats are intelligently designed. They have the ability to shift their balance as soon as they are airborne. Incredibly, their body determines which side should be up. Then, their ears and eyes direct their head to that position, followed by their spine, front feet, and hind legs. Like the landing gear of an incoming plane, their leg joints act as shock absorbers, set for their body's weight. The cat's backbone is extremely flexible, possessing 30 vertebrae. That's more than a human! Each ear of a feline has a built-in GPS feature called a vestibular system, which transmits to the cat where its body is in relation to the ground.

Did you know that anytime a cat is off its feet, it can reorient itself and regain its balance almost immediately from any position? It is even more fascinating that a cat can perform that function after being born for only six weeks without even being taught!

Recently, we received two furry felines into our home. Well, actually, I was the standalone vote against the measure in our family's Senate floor proceedings. Even when I attempted to filibuster the bill, I failed miserably. *"They're here already!"* Thus, the bill became law. Two cats! After doing some research, I must admit that I have a deeper appreciation for their running, jumping, pawing, and climbing. They are winners against a fatal form of adversity.

I know people who seem to come out ahead whenever they experience calamity consistently. Similar to cats, it's as if they have some kind of system for winning. Following are a few personal observations of how they win against adversity:

First, let's consider **truthfulness**. It is an invaluable tool. Being able to evaluate a personal situation honestly is an indispensable characteristic. That is critical because we must be able to identify whether we may be part of the problem, which is not always an easy task. Sometimes, the hardest thing to admit to ourselves is that we caused a negative consequence. Often, we develop internal mechanisms that prevent us from seeing the truth about ourselves. That is called "building walls" or "denial." Taking ownership of a personal problem can be a little painful, but you should have that ability if you are really serious about winning against adversity. You must be able to be honest about yourself with yourself.

Many years ago, it was not easy for me to tell that my decisions were terrible, even though the wreckage was all around me. Somehow, my sight was impaired when it came to my own deficiencies. Even when I could get them in my sights, I realized I lacked the level of resolve needed to face them. Before I knew it, they were out of sight again. My own denial concealed my imperfections…again.

One of the sensors that triggered defense mechanisms for me was pain. When you sprain an ankle, you don't have to remind yourself to limp. Your body will instinctively protect itself from further injury by causing you to put less pressure on the injured limb. Of course, the shooting pain is also a strong reminder. In fact, you must try to make yourself ignore that injury in order to try to walk or run normally. Something similar happens when you get hurt emotionally. You may suppress or hide the events from yourself for protection against further pain.

I used to tow a long line of bad decisions behind me, much like those old, loud, rusty railcars we used to see. All connected to that first train was me. Everyone could plainly see the steel boxcars (the decisions I made). Everyone, that is, except me. Why? Because of the pain that came with them. For a long time, I wondered whether it was that I couldn't see them or was it that I wouldn't see them. I now understand I wouldn't for so long that eventually, I couldn't.

Give me a second or two to discuss something called conscience. Conscience is the inner sense of what is right or wrong in one's conduct or motives, impelling them toward right action. Conscience is a very sensitive component in the human machine. It can eventually be reprogrammed to the standard code of the individual. It can also help you determine right or wrong and relative truth. For example, pilots fly by using their instruments in the cockpit, even when they are turned upside down. Conscience can be used to operate your life morally when it is turned topsy-turvy, although, through persistence, it can also be turned off.

There is another unique component involved during those times of self-denial we have not talked about yet. They are called "people" (i.e., mortals, humanoids, earthlings, homo sapiens—you and me). You may be saying, *"Okay. Admittedly I struggle with being honest with myself, but I want to win in this area."* You, my friend, are a champion! I have good news for you! Let me explain.

There will always be a person (usually someone close to you) who doesn't mind pouring a generous amount of verbal hydrogen peroxide into that open wound of yours. You may wince with discomfort, but hopefully, you will eventually see and accept a difficult truth. Truth be told, those types of people are invaluable. It's wise for you to keep them close.

Occasionally, we struggle with being honest with ourselves because of plain old immaturity. That also occurs among those who struggle with addiction. At the time a person becomes addicted, they stop progressing emotionally, while their age advances numerically. If you are going to win against adversity consistently, you must learn to be honest with yourself and continue to grow. Now, I am not saying you must be 100% honest about everything 24 hours a day. I am saying that you have to learn to be honest with yourself, or at least let someone help you move in that direction.

Without the characteristics of honesty, you can prolong the effects of misfortune. How? Well, first of all, when you can't get honest about your role in your own adversity, you can't take responsibility for its repercussions. Therefore, if you don't accept the consequences' weight, you might try to find someone who will. That is futile because almost no one assumes the obligation to take responsibility for something you "imagined" they did.

Secondly, if some aspect of a calamity is your fault and you don't correct your missteps, you will probably repeat those missed steps because you can't accept that they exist or that there is a need to overcome them. In fact, if you're looking for the root of an issue in the wrong place, you are probably spending all kinds of time, resources, and energy doing pointless things.

Another characteristic that people who consistently win against adversity seem to demonstrate is they have developed **patience**. A verse in the Book of Proverbs says, *"Patience can be developed in the midst of hardships."* Now, when I say patience, I am not talking about twiddling your fingers while you sit in a comfortable chair on the front porch. That's more like waiting or wishing. I am not talking about simply waiting. I am talking about how you wait. In other words, what is the quality of your attitude while you wait?

One of the ways my patience is tested in this area is check-out time at the supermarket. I seem to always get in the slowest line or the one that slows down and stops as soon as I get in it. Maybe that happens to you, too. As for me, it doesn't matter which store. I find a way to choose a line that is training a new cashier—one who must call the manager frequently.

When I first pick "that line," I do so based on the fact that it was moving the fastest. Other times, I've gotten into the line with the person who was making their very first purchase with a debit card, and maybe they get it right the fourth or fifth time. The test of my patience will usually kick in right after the line has come to a standstill for seven to ten minutes.

As you assess your patience level, observe your thoughts—and your body language. Do you think any of the following?

"It's going to be alright. It's probably their first day, and it just happens to be very busy."

"Hey, I remember when I got my first job. I didn't know everything that first day."

"These situations can put a lot of pressure on a person. I remember being very nervous."

That is the voice of patience.

On the other hand, I recall times when I thought:

"I'm sick of this! Every time I come here, this happens!"

"I'm already late. Why did they have to train this person today?"

"I should just go to another store."

"Maybe I'll talk to the manager. Maybe I'll talk to the district manager."

"Hello, somebody! I'm a paying customer!"

Those everyday life situations have a way of measuring our patience. If you don't think you have much patience, what can you do? Start by trying to think differently. When you find yourself in a situation where you must wait for something you want, change the way you think.

*"Did I give myself enough time?"*

*"What's the worst thing that could happen if I'm a little late?"*

*"Is there any way I could adjust my schedule to make up for lost time?"*

Asking yourself questions like those will prevent you from being negative and developing a bad attitude in situations that demand patience. Then, try putting yourself in another person's shoes by imagining what they are going through during the time you must wait. Those suggestions may sound strange, but they are little things that will help you become more patient. Patience is essential in overcoming the storms of adversity.

Here's something else that is important in winning against adversity: **emotional stability**. We all have emotions, both positive and negative. We were created with them, so they are meant to be experienced. However, we must be able to manage them instead of having them manage us.

For instance, it is normal to encounter disappointment during times of adversity. After all, misfortune is probably not what we expected to show up at our door when it did. Initially, we are faced with a sense of hopelessness. That is when it is easy to slip into depression—something that can happen to any of us. When we experience depression caused by adversity, we must remind ourselves that it will pass. Most often, that heavy feeling subsides, and when it doesn't, we should probably make ourselves talk to someone about it. Depression caused by misfortune cannot always be stopped from visiting us, but don't let it hang around long enough to rent a room.

It is possible to set boundaries for negative emotions. At most, give yourself to the end of the day and then release them. They should fuel you, not rule you. Let negative emotions energize you to move in a positive direction. A person who has emotional stability can experience negative emotions and still move forward. It's not always easy, but in order to win against adversity, you must accept your emotions—positive and negative—experience them, and get your focus back to success in your life. Don't let the highs take you too high, and never let the lows take you too low. Try to remain somewhere in the middle.

I know. Easier said than done, right? That's because we don't start on a level playing field. There is a great misconception when we prejudge people, and it is this: We don't understand that everyone doesn't start at ground zero. Some people started in front of the pack by being born into wealth or political power. Many other people just started out normal with an average family, life, and social status. Then, there are some who started out in the negative. Those people came into the world already behind others in one way or another. So, it is unwise to judge others simply because you don't know what it took for them to reach "normal."

Life is sometimes like trying to win that big stuffed teddy bear at the arcade in an amusement park. Areas of our lives may seem easy to win at first glance. Then, we find ourselves struggling to win once we begin. We experience bad friendships, disrespectful bosses, and lackadaisical coworkers. There are irrational landlords and insensitive loved ones. Each situation seems perfectly normal initially, but we soon find ourselves thinking, *"I just can't win!"*

In our fight to sustain our emotional stability, we may have suffered some emotional wounds. For our emotions to become stable, they must first be normalized again. When our emotions become severely damaged, we may require a skilled professional's assistance to help us on our journey to emotional health. Then, when adversity comes, we will be positioned to advance and win.

Another trait that those who consistently win against adversity exhibit is **discipline**. When I say discipline, I mean self-control. Self-control is defined as control of one's emotions, desires, actions, etc. We are all human. Most of us, at some time or another, allow our self-control to get away from us. Nobody is perfect. The wrong circumstances at the wrong time could cause anyone to have a momentary lapse in judgment. If you work at trying to keep yourself (your emotions, desires, and actions) under control, you can get better.

Discipline is invaluable when facing adversity. Amid your circumstances being turned upside down, you must stay right-side up. When you are faced with prolonged adversity, one of the thoughts that seem to linger is, *"When will this be over?"* Whether it is emotional, financial, or physical, there is usually some pain attached. Most people don't like pain, especially when it lingers. As such, what we want most once calamity has begun is for it to end.

Where am I going with all of this? A lack of self-control can compound the situation, making the time of adversity seem as if it will never end.

It is challenging to have no control over a negative circumstance while, at the same time, trying to get control over yourself. While lacking self-control emotionally, your feelings will attempt to lead you. They will try to dictate over you and want to define you. With no self-control spiritually, you have no inner compass and may lack the ability to differentiate between right and wrong or the courage to choose it. If you have little self-control financially, you will constantly be digging yourself out of a hole you should have never climbed into. In the social arena, with no self-control, you may find yourself spending most of your spare time with those you only feel comfortable with but have no way of helping you climb to another level. When you have little or no self-control physically, you may allow your fitness level to diminish, resulting in permanent damage and pain. Without self-control sexually, you could find yourself with a defective reputation, in a miserable relationship, or worse. Discipline (or self-control) is absolutely vital in winning against adversity.

The last characteristic I will discuss is **maturity**. I mentioned its importance earlier when I mentioned being honest with ourselves. To one degree or another, there is probably a little child in all of us. Sometimes, we just want to act playful and have fun. Occasional frivolity is normal behavior.

One of the definitions of the word maturity in its noun form means "mental competence or mental fitness; also, well developed." In other words, your mind is in good shape. You workout. You have a reasonable ability to make your mind do what you want it to do. To win against adversity, you will need to work on your mental fitness actively. In fact, adversity is sometimes like an obstacle course. You must constantly be thinking in order to advance.

Some people are young in numerical age, but they already seem to have a certain level of maturity, meaning mental fitness. Maybe it is because of genetics, but it might also be because of hard work and exercise. On some occasions, you will find a person older in years that is still very immature. Even with added years, some have not worked on exercising their mind. We can all become mentally out of shape. So then, maturity can fluctuate depending on the individual. That does not automatically have to parallel a person's numerical age. Today, we decide to mature and get in shape.

There are many venues in life where we will be challenged by adversity. But how do you know if you are winning or not? Let me conclude this chapter with a few pieces of evidence we should discover while we win. Let's consider winning at its essence. It is to succeed by effort or ability; to gain a victory.

First of all, we can know that we are winning against adversity because we are still succeeding personally during it. You may have wealth, great relationships, and a respectable career. But you as a person could still be losing the battle. We all know inwardly (regardless of our circumstances) When we are improving, developing, learning, and gaining new territory. We can have this kind of success during our experience with adversity.

Secondly, if you are winning against adversity, an effort has been made. It doesn't matter what kind of competition it is, you can rarely win without an effort. Intense adversity has the capacity to paralyze us initially. We get that alarming feeling like being stuck on a Ferris wheel. We go around and around, buckled in tightly to that situation, with no one to turn off the ride. The switch to turn the power off those uncontrolled, reoccurring thoughts is your own effort. Just start. Start to think. Start to grieve. Start to heal. And never be afraid to dream another dream. You may need to ask God for help.

The last piece of evidence we find at the scene of a person winning against adversity is skill and ability. That is where resources like this book are vital. They equip us with a playbook for the game and the skills necessary to compete.

Utilize available resources that coincide with your experience to develop your ability. You may be in adversity or coming out of it. That is a great time to develop a new ability.

Adversity is an opponent we will all have to face many, many times in our lives. You have a winning record in competitions when you have won more than you have lost. At various times while we are here on this earth, we must match up against adversity. We will meet it in all its efforts, talents, and ability. We simply aspire to win more than we lose.

Now, start your engine, then carefully check all your gauges. Now go ahead and step on that gas pedal. Rev it up a few times. That is the sound and feel of your new, enhanced life engine. Get ready to dominate your next race against adversity!

# Chapter Six
# Seven Laws of Advancing Through Adversity

An aerial panoramic of my life depicts a wide array of adversity. Some are small, and some are great. Some are short, and some are long. Some healed overnight, while many have left deep scars. Through it all, though, by God's grace, today I soar!

I have researched, studied adversity, examined my personal experiences, and reached out to those in misfortune. I have conversed with several friends with whom I have much in common. I have concluded that certain principles, like scientific laws, consistently occur when certain conditions exist or are met.

Well, here they are: **Seven Laws of Advancing Through Adversity.**

The first law deals with **strength**. Develop inner strength before trouble comes because it tests you. A diamond is really processed by two elements: heat and pressure. The weight of adversity reveals how strong you are internally in the same way working out in the gym demonstrates your physical side. Those two sides of strength don't necessarily come as a package deal. Like Martin Luther King, Jr., Helen Keller, and Gandhi, many people were powerful weightlifters on the inside but maybe weren't much in the gym.

The second law speaks of **endurance**. Advancing through adversity is a process, not a sprint. So, don't time it; endure it. Rock climbing in triathlons requires tremendous endurance. Similarly, advancing through adversity will require a strategy, hard work, and determination. Don't become preoccupied or fixated with a particular situation, wondering every day when it will be over. Just keep getting up every morning. If you need adjustments, then make them. But keep moving forward. Don't quit. Prolonged frustration brings discouragement, and continued discouragement entices you to give up. Just keep fighting. You have just one more round to go. Visualize it. See yourself reaching the goal, enjoying the fruits of your labor. Verbalize it. Speak positive things about yourself. Your ears need to hear your mouth, saying, "I am moving forward." Be advised: allow those who are trusted friends to share their opinions. Then, start. Before you know it, you will make it through the toughest part. Then, you develop momentum. Now, just keep following that direction.

      The third law underscores the word **loyalty**. Trouble and adversity define the loyalty of those around you. Some people with whom you can never really determine their level of personal commitment until you experience trouble and adversity. The word loyalty means "devoted, reliable, and true." Adversity in trouble may uncover the fact that some people in your life are not reliable and true when you need them the most. A strong supporting cast can make or break a person's ability to go through adversity. Choose your personal teammates in life wisely. You may have to depend on them sooner or later.

      The fourth law focuses on **change**. Adversity can be a change agent, so don't resist a positive exchange. Have you ever reversed sides from where you usually sit at lunch, only to find new people you have everything in common with? Maybe you've tried switching up the way you normally drive to school or church and realize it was faster. You might have recently substituted a new product for one you often use and realize that somehow, you feel better. Those are all examples of changes that produce positive exchange.

## Overcome Your Storm, Rebuild Your Hope

I wonder what life would be like if we randomly said, *"I think I'll change today. For no particular reason, I am just going to move several things around in my life."* It would be interesting, but it's not very likely to happen. The serious changes we make in life are usually the aftermath of something or someone causing us deep introspection. In fact, it's usually when we are forced to that we make the most significant changes. When adversity comes, anticipate change. Many times, those changes are for the better. A valuable exchange will leave you with a profit after its conclusion. Learn to embrace them.

The fifth law uses the word **companions**. Adversity usually travels with some companions; hurt, hope, and heal. Don't be intimidated by them. As a result of experiencing adversity, at some point, we may experience some form of pain. Even though we don't always like to admit it, most of us get hurt often. It's normal to experience pain, but it can become counterproductive. Be careful not to allow pain to rent out a room in your mind and stay as long as it wants. Just tell it, *"Hey! Your lease is up. You have to move!"* When you feel hurt, find hope, and then pursue healing. Many people get hurt while experiencing adversity but never cross over to hope. Platinum Hope is a strong, fortified desire, accompanied by a bold, almost arrogant expectation of obtaining what you desire. When you get hurt, expect yourself to overcome that hurt. That is hope, and it will help you on your journey to healing.

The sixth law speaks of **favoritism**. Adversity does not discriminate, so don't take it personally. Don't let yourself fall into self-pity. It will squeeze the emotional life right out of you. When you take adversity too personally, it can produce self-pity. It is okay to evaluate the adversity you are facing to find its origin. Is it because of your own negligence?

Recently, I stopped at a gas station with multiple islands to gas up my car. I pulled in just before another car. The young man went right over to the other car first. *"Hmm,"* I thought. *"I must be invisible."* I was perturbed and perplexed, but not without theory. *"He did that on purpose,"* I said to myself. I don't usually allow that kind of thing to bother me, but that particular time, I chose to address it. *"Didn't you see me here first?"*

*"Yeah. Did you want diesel?"* came his reply.

Don't personalize adversity. Most people in life are not out to get you. Trouble harasses all types of people, regardless of race, sex, religion, or economic status. The vehicles adversity uses may differ, but trouble reaches us all.

The seventh law zeroes in on the word **promotion**. If you learn from trouble and adversity, they will promote you. To promote means to raise someone to a higher position or rank. Hard work, training, knowing the right people, and perfect scores are all thoughts that come to mind when we think of the word promotion. But you probably never thought adversity could promote you, right? You can indeed be raised to a higher place through adversity. Adversity provides new lessons for you and about you. If you are personally willing to learn while you are going through adversity, you will be at a higher place as you exit. The quality of your character can improve. You will also grow and mature. The result of the promotion is fantastic, even if the road you travel to get there was a little unusual.

## *Between Flights*

So far, we have discussed adversity in various aspects. Now, we understand there is a way to overcome adversity and let it work for you. Yes, adversity can be overcome. Its lessons can be learned and accredited. In the second half of this manual, we will discuss rebuilding hope. In life, we can overcome adversity, as well as rebuild our hope after the storm. Adversity and hope are two separate spheres that, like planets, don't just cosmically connect and strike up a conversation. When we wrestle with misfortune or calamity, we can wear ourselves out. That's usually the hardest time to dream.

As we approach the intersection of this book, I am reminded of an experience. I absolutely love slicing through jumbo clouds on commercial flights. There is only one thing more breathtaking than the view and feel of being close enough to a cloud that I can hear it breathing. I've listened to some of my friends, but for me, the part of flying I find the most enjoyable is ascending and descending. The takeoff is like climbing a colossal stairway while watching the objects beneath slowly become pleasantly unrecognizable. On the other hand, once the airliner begins tobogganing, the landscape is unparalleled.

Imagine watching from an aerial view a huge abstract painting hundreds of feet beneath you. As you descend, your eyes begin zooming and autofocus with pinpoint resolution. Suddenly, you can appreciate the tapestry of colors, shades, shapes, and lines as they are being transformed into an actual real-life American skyline, like Washington DC, Denver, or Las Vegas, complete with an assortment of humans. That is amazing! Now, you land in that city and are shuffled off the plane and rest at Terminal B.

You have come to the part of the trip you have been trying not to think about. It is the layover. *"It was the only way to get this flight on such short notice,"* you keep telling yourself convincingly. So, there you are. You have traveled through time zones. The flight has taken you across mountains, oceans, and tiny villages snuggled together in deep valleys. You have flown low enough to see squirrels feasting on treetops and high enough to feel your ears pop like a cork freed from an old wine bottle. So, use that time to reflect on the journey while considering the destination.

That's where we are in this literary excursion—somewhere in between two flights. You thought there was time to visit the gift shop and grab a newspaper. Then, the green light flickers on earlier than you expected, accompanied by a welcoming voice.

*"Now boarding at Gate 4: Rebuilding Your Hope- Section 2!"*

Let's go! Hurry!

# Part 2:
# Rebuild Your Hope

## Chapter Seven
## What Is Hope?

What is hope? Well, let's begin by talking about what hope is not. Hope is not throwing a quarter in the water fountain at the mall, closing your eyes, and thinking about something you want. That is called A wish. Hope is not thinking a good opportunity is going to happen while you sit in a lawn chair in the backyard, waiting for it to fall in your lap. That is called a pipe dream. Hope is not silently walking by the desk of a single, attractive coworker, year after year, thinking, *"Today, they will notice me."* That is called an allusion.

The brand of hope I am talking about is **Platinum Hope**. Platinum hope is intense desire superglued to an unbreakable expectation of obtaining the goal. When you really hope for something, you fully expect to obtain it. Hope is very similar to other words we use, like passion, dream, and vision. Hope is that thing we dreamed about in elementary school and talked about in junior high. We then became informed about it and formally participated in it during our high school and young adult years, if not sooner. Most of us chose something to hope for or had our hopes passed onto us by our parents. Either way, in our youth, we developed hope for something we fully expected to obtain. We may have been slightly naive in our dreams, but we still held on to them.

I had a very vibrant hope that stayed with me from early childhood all the way up until high school. Then, I allowed another human being to crack open my soul like a safe and burglarize my hope. It was a great heist, indeed.

I still remember being a fifth-grader the night before Christmas. I was excited about my gifts, but I noticed a tiny sprig of coolness peak up from under the soil of my adolescence just a few days prior. As colorful lights in windows take turns reciting their blink, my mind asserted a command. *"Boy, you better run down those stairs! It's Christmas!"* I peeped out my bedroom door to see if the security (which was my parents) had clocked out for the night. I could see something unusual, something unexpected. I had to get a closer look. It was a pretty good-sized box. Whatever the gift was, it wasn't wrapped. Cautiously standing halfway down the stairs with my little hand clenched tightly to a handcrafted banister, I could clearly see a label on the side of the box. It was a 110-pound weight set!

"I don't remember asking for this one, but I am more excited about this gift than anything else."

"This has to be from my dad."

"I can't wait to use these!"

"This is going to help me a lot where I'm going in life."

"I have to get a lot stronger."

"I'm going to workout every day."

"Now, I can stop buying all that bubble gum to get the girls' attention."

"They will probably all dump their boyfriends and start liking me after I get done pumping iron!" I remember the idea of "pumping iron" exciting me so much, I didn't even realize what I actually had was mustard-brown, vinyl-covered, round, donut-styled plates. To me, I had iron. And my dad? He's the best!

A few years later, I remember being approached by some of the high school athletes. Since I had started lifting weights, I also started having fun with some friends in my neighborhood. Each street represented a different team. During those years, I also worked on speed and agility. When I was young and engrossed in something, the way my friends and I were, we didn't really care if, when, or by whom we were being watched, unless, of course, we were being watched by a girl.

Two of the top high school varsity players waited for me after one of our street games. *"We want you to be our equipment manager,"* they said. Equipment manager was another name for the water boy. I had no misconceptions about that respected invitation. It was well known in our sports tradition that that selection was deliberate. An adolescent that an entire varsity team and its coaches agreed would spend time around them at practices, on team buses, at games, and in the locker room, usually meant one thing. It meant there was potential for that young person to develop into a serious athlete. I actually thought it was a prank initially. Unbelievably, it was real.

The pre-teen crown jewel came a year later after I graduated from Hopkins Middle School. I was sternly told to be at the pre-summer camp. That was about pure dedication. It started only a couple of days after school let out for the summer. It was also before the traditional, mandatory two-a-day summer practices began. There were no coaches, no equipment, and no glory. It was just heart, sweat, veterans, and my cleats. By the time our freshman year began, my mind was made up. I had thought about it for the last couple of years. I loved the game. I was good and would only get better. Football is what I would choose to do with my life. High school, college, and then pro. During my junior year, a well-respected athletic associate looked me right in the eyes and said, *"You are too small to play at that level!"* Those carefully placed words attacked my hope of a football career like a deadly virus. In a couple of days, my dream was lifeless. No pulse. No breathing. No brain activity. It simply flatlined.

Over the years, many people have had their hopes and dreams abducted. Many times, the culprit has been adversity. Some people have gone through intense battles with adversity, turned around suddenly, and realized that something was missing. Their hopes, dreams, and goals were nowhere to be found.

Okay. So, you had certain goals before misfortune and trouble showed up, and you realize you dropped those goals. Maybe like me, adversity spoke to you audibly: *"You will never be able to..."* Hold it! That is something that belongs to you! Don't let adversity boss you around!

Understand that adversity can't really take your hope, nor is it actually trying to. When adversity comes, it brings pressure. When we sense pressure, our minds tell us it would be easier to release the hope and just face the adversity. Remember this: A dream delayed does not equal a dream denied. Just go back to the drawing board. Reconstruct, adjust, maneuver, and find a way.

Your hopes, dreams, visions, and passions are a gift from God. They are valuable, so get them and hold onto them. Be determined and tenacious because the greater the hope is, the stronger the adversity you may face and the deeper the impact it may have in your life. If we are going to see our dreams become a reality, we must prepare for the fight and protect our hope.

I have a cousin who is a few years older than me. His name is Kevin. He was an extremely successful athlete. He was a three-time New Jersey State Champion. The local wrestlers in the high school I attended maintained a bitter crosstown rivalry with his. However, they held him in very high regard. Many years after high school, I remembered his success. During that time in my life, I had built new dreams and goals. I was on the slow road to recovery from wrestling with my own slice of adversity. I recall humbly approaching him and asking sincerely but directly, *"How did you become so successful in wrestling? You achieved greatness!"*

*"Every time I stepped on the mat, I learned a new move,"* he replied.

What a winning mindset! To me, the match was his tutor. Win, lose, or draw, I get better!

We will have a similar approach during adversity, once we have decided to contend with realizing the dream, vision, or hope. So, don't let adversity be the reason you give up your hope. Instead, let it teach you a new move.

Hope can also be appraised by what it conceives in someone else. It could release a chain reaction in the lives of 20 or 30 other people. Just because they see you rebuilding your hope, it could inspire them to begin rebuilding theirs. Often, when someone does something negative, people imitate that. We understand that positive events can have the same effect. So, after the storm is over, assess the damage, retool, and rebuild. Roll up those sleeves and put your work clothes on. Do whatever you have to do to get those creative juices flowing. Once realized, your hope may touch someone who discovers a scientific breakthrough for our environment or someone who becomes an emergency medical technician who saves lives. Your hope—that desire you have to do something that you are completely convinced will happen—may inspire someone whose calling is working with abused children.

Overcome Your Storm, Rebuild Your Hope

We must do all we can to keep our hopes and dreams right where they belong—on the inside of you and me—until they are developed enough to be released.

This book is going to touch the lives of many people from various walks of life. Across this country, even across the globe, men and women, young and old, rich and not so rich, will be able to identify not just with overcoming adversity but with the process of renovating those old dreams and goals after the storm. This book will nudge people. People like you and me.

I had goals, hopes, and desires before adversity came into my life. When all the dust had settled, I didn't have the same desire to pursue those dreams. I wouldn't be writing this book if it weren't for people who dared me to spread my wings and soar! Those people inspired me to reach for greatness, for which I am extremely grateful. I am still reaching.

What is **Platinum Hope**? Platinum is a chemical element with the atomic number 78 on the periodic table. It is a precious metal found deep in the earth's crust. Platinum is dense and malleable, which means it can be shaped by heat and pressure. It is also transitional, so it can easily adapt from one form to another. The element is also categorized as a precious metal, which means it is very costly. Platinum also exhibits a remarkable resistance to corrosion, wear, and tarnish. Its rarity causes those in marketing to associate it with exclusivity in wealth. Platinum Hope is a human element. It is produced in the soul, can be shaped into various forms, can withstand pressure and heat, and is very costly. Platinum Hope is an upgraded format of normal hope.

In today's times, people need an enhanced version of hope. So much violence in our country stems from the absence of hope or what is known as hopelessness. Our hope, dream, or vision must be more intense, resilient, and intentional in this age. We must locate our hope, fight for it, and never quit. A wise man once said to me, *"Life is a series of quitting points."* It is true we all have many opportunities and incentives to pull the plug on our own hope. This manual will help equip us to persist.

In my teen years, I faced nine assassins. Forces contracted to murder my hope in cold blood. At the age of ten, I was sexually abused by a non-family member. By age 11, it was cigarettes. By the time I was 13, I was drinking alcohol. At the age of 14, I was introduced to marijuana. Once I turned 15, I was hanging out in the streets and nightclubs. My 16th birthday was followed by an invitation to try cocaine, which I accepted. At 17, I was already a promiscuous street hustler, and by the time I was 23, I was a drug addict. Through the power of God, my life has gone from plastic to Platinum.

From as early as I can remember, my father scattered seeds of entrepreneurship over my young soul. Now that the smoke has cleared, I am living the definition of **Platinum Hope**.

# Chapter Eight
# The Value of Hope

Dressed in plaid shorts in a button-down, short-sleeve shirt, a young man burst onto the escalator. He had a cool posture, but it was obvious his thoughts raced like sports cars through traffic lights. His hair was styled and lubricated, with each braid standing in tight formation. He topped off his look with the latest sneakers, their pride being the neon pigmentation. One thought permeated his young, determined mind: *"Today, I am going to do it."* There was an irrefutable expression on the face of that young man in his condition. His sincere eyes, dancing smile, an undaunted swag seemed to radiate a certain fearlessly pleasant pursuit of something. As he strode across the marble floor, several vendors take notice. His cool attempt at self-control is futile. It reminded me of someone trying to hold a small party balloon underwater. His excitement just kept resurfacing. *"I am really down for this,"* he reassures himself.

As he got closer to his destination, his palms began to secrete buckets of sweat. The collaborative rhythm of heartbeats and breaths rose their tempo. He then blurted out, *"There it is!"* Suddenly, he contemplated the first part of the summer break. *"Yo, I've been working at this bookstore all summer and every break for two years,"* he mused. *"I worked mad hours every chance I had. I've been grinding for real!"*

*"Hello, sir. What brings you into our store today?"* the keen, young saleswoman queries.

*"It's ring time. Show me something expensive,"* he says.

*"She must mean a lot,"* the saleswoman replied.

*"Yes, she does. She's invaluable."*

Let's talk about the value of hope because hope has great value. The word value is defined as "estimated or appraised worth." Someone's appraisal of an object or even another person can differ based on their perceived estimation. For example, the young man at the mall was obviously excited about making a critical declaration. He stated clearly why he was looking for something so extravagant for his soon-to-be fiancé. The reason was she is priceless. Her worth to him is appraised high enough to demand planning, employment, budgeting, and hopes of a happily ever after.

So, what is the estimated value of a person's hope, dream, or desire? one way to estimate the value or worth of something is to envision its greatest potential. What could it become if the proper conditions are met? Potential is what is possible but has not yet been developed.

Let's now talk about acorns and caterpillars. Acorns are small and brown, with no particular pattern or great design to its shell. There's nothing out of the ordinary concerning their shape. They are very basic and round. Have you ever driven down the street and observed what appeared to be a small river of acorns? They are uneventful, unassuming, and plain. That describes the acorn's personality. You probably never heard another human being plead with the driver of an automobile to halt so that he could get a closer look at the acorns. You are probably a lot more familiar with the sound of their crunch under a trundling tire.

However, did you know that by crushing one acorn, you could be destroying a whole forest? That is because one acorn can produce hundreds of trees. Even though it took only one acorn to create that gargantuan hardwood, dangling from its limbs are hundreds of acorns. So, guess what each one of those nuts could become? Exactly. It could become another tree.

Besides a squirrel or its kin, one other species gets excited about acorns. It is the Oak tree. The Oak tree understands the worth of an acorn. To most people, the value of an acorn is not very high. We just don't see much use for it. But to the Oak tree itself, the acorn is viewed much differently. Maybe the proud Oak sees his lineages. The tree would probably smile if it could, as it watches a baby acorn fall and snuggle its way into the soil. Over the months, it matures into a tender young sapling. The family name lives on.

I remember in the neighborhood where I grew up, there were many trees in our yard. They were also smaller shrubs. At certain times of the year, those trees and shrubs were elegantly adorned with leaves. As the months passed, we observed the shedding of their sunbaked foliage. When I looked closely at the trees' bark, I would discover schools of caterpillars. Some were black or Brown; others were green. They were all covered with hairy whiskers. They moved gracefully and methodically. They were subtle, almost unnoticeable. The worst thing to see was the death of a caterpillar. When someone would step on one of the woolly bears, you would see whiskers, its curled little body, and a green fluid.

While growing up, I remember one kid who actually attempted to capture one of the larvae in a shoebox, take it home, and domesticate it. Of course, when he got home, his plan was met with swift, considerable opposition. A promise of severe punishment followed that if the situation was not rectified immediately.

For the most part, caterpillars can be fun. Initially, caterpillars are interesting to observe. However, most of us would conclude that they don't appear to have any redeeming quality or excitement after a short period of time. An average person may look at a caterpillar and joke, *"One day, that ugly thing will be a butterfly,"* as they smirk and snicker. A unique person may actually envision a beautiful butterfly as they stare at that ugly Caterpillar. Only a rare, gifted, or skilled individual could imagine a Five-Winged Morpho A. Aurora X Eugenia — the most expensive butterfly in the world. It is worth between $100,000 and $200,000 and can only be found in Peru or Bolivia. It actually has a fifth underdeveloped wing! It is extremely rare. Maybe one out of a million people could determine a five-winged Morpho in its caterpillar stage.

      The potential value or worth of a person rebuilding their hope or reaching a dream is immeasurable. Every person has a hope or a dream at some point in their life. One young lady always dreamed of becoming a racecar driver. Another individual could have always hoped to become a doctor. Once realized, that hope could bring them into a state of financial wealth that could secure a very stable future for generations to come. Another person could have a lifelong desire to travel to a foreign country and aid those left in the aftermath of a natural disaster. What do you think the people in that country would say the worth of that person was? "Priceless" would probably be their response. What about the young boy whose dream has always been to become a firefighter one day? Unfortunately, somewhere in a small suburb, a family is about to be deprived of almost everything they own in a raging fire. Reluctantly, they watch what used to be their home now being devoured. Suddenly, they realized that their cherished family pet (their cat Sasha) is missing. Then, they look up and see an embattled firefighter. Wouldn't you know, it is that same little boy with a crazy dream? Except now, he is the man emerging through the smoke and charred wood with their cat in his arms. What do you think his childhood dream of being a firefighter is worth now?

Those special people reached their goals, but their goals began as just a hope, a dream, and a desire. Now, maybe it becomes a little clear. As we discussed the value of hope, we began to distinguish another part of its significance. We understand that hope's accurate appraisal is not only based on the person who has it but also on those it may benefit. After we are gone, the legacy we leave on this planet will have more to do with the latter.

Let me be clear and direct: Someone needs the gift that you will become. One of the noblest passions a human being can have is to serve others intentionally. It should be humbling, not arrogant, to think that someone's life could be enhanced by the fulfillment of the dream in you. No matter what attitude you may have about yourself, the value of your dream is real.

We all have a dream inside of us. We all have gifts and talents. We have some alike, and many that are different. But we all have them. It is a healthy attitude that says the gifts we have are not just for our personal enjoyment. Yes, I know that there are people whose focus is only on themselves and what their gift or talent provides for them alone. I won't be critical, except to say that their view is somewhat narrow. The potential of human beings is vast. However, that potential can also be walled in by our own minds.

I remember years ago, I heard a great man speak about acrophobia, which is the fear of Heights. He was speaking from a spiritual perspective. His point was punctual for me, in particular. *"We can't be afraid to fly together,"* he sermonized. That had a lot to do with what we were born to do. Turkeys can fly, but they do it very differently than Eagles. The key is understanding your gifts and talents, which, by the way, are uniquely yours.

Sometimes, we get so caught up in comparisons. Unfortunately, when we do that, we delete the fact that some of our effectiveness is locked up in our own uniqueness.

There are times in life when you're not hovering at ground level, and you're also not soaring through the clouds. You are somewhere in the middle. Do you ever feel like things are going well in a particular endeavor, and you are comfortable where you are? Except there's just one thing: You don't feel satisfied. You think that there is more.

There are times we feel as if there are unique aspects of our lives that are not being utilized. We then wake up in the morning, and there is an ensemble of dormant skills and gifts singing loudly and on key.

*"Good morning, man! We are here, and we are ready,"* they resound.

Good can definitely become the rivalry of your best. If you feel that way often, maybe it is your time to fly higher. That special hope that is in human beings is of infinite value. I believe so strongly that after overcoming the storms of adversity, which most of us will do many times, it is important to reexamine our hope.

I have a friend who is a homeowner's insurance adjuster. His job is to help homeowners review and understand the provisions of the policy. He also helps them estimate the cost of repairs.

The storms of life can be complex. They can destroy large chunks of our dreams. Then, at other times, those massive storms of adversity can almost flit by and barely graze us. Either way, after adversity's past, it is important to estimate the impact the storm has had on our purpose. As much as it may feel like during a storm that it is a good time to quit, it probably isn't. It is almost like a family living in a beautiful home, the front porch gets damaged by a tornado, and the family decides to abandon the home. There is one big financial reason why a family who paid off and now owns their home is probably not going to get rid of it just because a few steps are missing.

There is also a huge reason why someone who has invested in a dream or vision over the years should not just up and vacate the premises of the thing they have always hoped to attain. The concept is very similar to both of those investments. It is called equity. We all know and understand that homes have equity. Basically, equity is the monetary value of a property beyond any amounts owed on a mortgage or loan. So, we know that homes have equity, but did you know that dreams have equity? That's right. It will cost you to build your dreams. You will have to give up something and possibly borrow something. However, your dream is valuable because one day, it will pay you in more ways than one. The price you had to pay to build and realize your dream will be offset by what it will produce in the long run. Whether it is a house you purchased or a dream you are endowed with, the great news is it's yours. You have sole ownership. You possess complete control over it. You can use it for many things or use them for very little. You can rent it, give it away, sell it, or just keep it for your personal enjoyment. The choice is yours. The value of a house appreciates or increases over time. The worth of the house is not important to the house itself. It increases the worth of those who own it. Likewise, the hope, dream, or vision has no worth to itself but produces value to the owner and their desired recipients. That is why it is important to assess what belongs to you after the storms of adversity have calmed.

One great, religious man in this country has counseled four presidents of the United States. Through his sermons, it is reported that over one million people have been converted to

Christianity. What price tag would you put on the hope and dreams he had as a young man to impact people's lives? We can evaluate a person's realized hope by its effect on those who have been touched by it. You can also see the value of hope on those who possess it.

I believe that one of the most satisfying feelings a human can experience is when a hope, dream, or goal is realized. It is so rewarding. One of the most significant points for me is knowing that I stuck with my decision. Usually, there are many, many opportunities to quit. When you persevere with hope or a commitment and decide to stick with it, it is very fulfilling. It is especially meaningful when you stick with it and succeed.

Something else in life that is also fascinating is being able to watch something grow. It may be a plant, a puppy, a tree, or a child. It is actually fun and very interesting. You can watch the stages of development. You mark the differences in your memory. When you have hope, dream, or desire, have been carrying it for a while, and you release it, it's similar to giving birth. It is a part of you. Then, the fun begins, and more pain, too. Just like you watching that child begin to grow, you can observe your hope, dream, or desire move from stage to stage. You superintend as your dream begins to crawl and then stand, walk, and eventually run. Soon, it will be able to function with less and less of your personal assistance. Fortunately, your hope will never turn 18, tell you it's grown and that it knows more than you, run off to college, get married without your permission, and have beautiful children.

The point I am making is that it is exciting and priceless to watch your hope grow and develop through every stage.

# Chapter Nine
# Rebuild Your Hope After the Storms of Adversity

Over the past decade, the United States has witnessed a sharp increase in severe storms causing incredible damage. The impact of the damage has been life-changing. The toll has been costly, including the deaths of loved ones, as well as affectionate pets that were never recovered. Then, there were automobiles, fishing boats, and sadly even homes lost.

One of the most amazing things to witness during the aftermath of a national disaster is to see people from diverse backgrounds come together. It's fascinating to see human beings cross anything in their path to help each other after a devastating storm. It is like a collective internal switch is turned on. Once activated, it's like nothing else matters, except rebuilding after the storm. Massive supplies are donated. Volunteers of endless manpower appear. Even ardent, sincere community prayer is offered. In the aftermath of a natural disaster, most people are eager not only to rebuild their own dream, but also the dreams of others.

The word rebuild denotes repairing or remodeling extensively by taking apart and reconstructing, often with new parts. Let me talk a little bit more about rebuilding your hope after the storm of adversity. The older I get, I seem to be reflecting more on my childhood growing up in LaGorce Square.

We loved homemade go-karts! The mention of those three words probably awakened volumes of carefree childhood endeavors. Riding go-karts was only half the fun. The other half was building them. Most of the kids in my neighborhood were far from poor. However, that did not mean that our parents would purchase every little thing we imagined would be cool to have. The fun part of growing up was learning that you can bring many ideas from your imagination into reality with a little determination and challenging work. It is said that necessity is the mother of invention. I would add that wanting something bad enough as a child, but knowing your parents weren't going to buy it, inspired its fair share of innovation as well.

There was a huge field behind my parents' house where I grew up. At one end of this huge, oblong field, there was a little cul-de-sac. In between the houses on the horseshoe-shaped street, there was a narrow path. There was also a sign there that read "Dead End." At the other end of the field were peach orchards, pear orchards, grapes, and blackberry trees that had been left unharvested. So, the slightly larger than a football field-sized acreage was nicknamed "The Dead End."

It was scarce in those days, but we could occasionally find small pockets of junk, but good junk. When we did find something salvageable, we erupted with *"Yeah, man!"* and gave each other high-fives. We celebrated like a bunch of old sea merchants hauling in the biggest catch of the day. Most of the time, we would have to search through the debris to find something we could really use. During the go-kart season, there were a few treasures that were at the top of the list. I'm hoping not to overdramatize this. I'm only talking about a few good friends meeting up a couple of times a week to have some good fun. Every so often, though, we would stumble upon the sacred items we could not do without. Those items were sturdy wood and working wheels.

Our process of go-kart manufacturing was pure inspiration. First, we would get a picture or vision in our head of what we wanted our individual karts to look like. Then, we would literally just find the parts and pieces that best match each of our concepts. Initially, there would need to be plywood. We needed two long, narrow 2' x 4' pieces of wood that we used as axles for the wheels. For steering, we would have to find some rope and cut it into two long pieces. Then, we would tie one end of one of the pieces of rope to the axle's left side. Next, we tied the other end of the other piece to the axle's right side, almost like pulling the left or right rein to cause a horse to steer right or left, while both pieces of rope were held in either hand. You could turn the wooden axle left or right once the wheels were attached by pulling the rope in the left hand or the right. Then came the tricky part. We needed nails, and they had to be straight ones, which we could rarely find in the field. All of our dads kept nails, screws, hammers, and other supplies in our garages. At our ages, though, those tools were off-limits to us. So, we would have to figure that part out by either asking politely or making up a story. Eventually, we were able to get what we needed. Once we had our nails, the project was brought to life.

With enthusiasm racing in our young souls, we would meet up at whoever's home had the best driveway with no cars parked in it. That is usually when we would face the quality control tests of our own craftsmanship. Often, in the beginning at least, there would be breakdowns, several crashes, and we'd occasionally end up on a neighbor's front lawn. We would then remodel, repair, and repeatedly rebuild until "We Ride."

That is what we do when the storms of adversity hit us. We rebuild until we ride.

We are still talking about a **PLATINUM** brand of hope, which is an intense desire super-glued to an unbreakable expectation of obtaining the goal. At some point in our lives—infancy, preteen, adolescence, or even young adulthood—our hope was discovered. It was discovered because it was there at birth or before. Life's circumstances can sink our hopes. Adversity can torpedo our dreams. Then, like priceless spoils in an old, wounded warship, hope slowly drifts to the ocean floor of our soul. But guess what? It is as valuable today, if not more, than the day it was submerged. It just needs to be recovered and restored.

Have you ever watched those treasure hunting shows or seen someone at a beach with a serious metal detector? You can tell they are engaging in an intense operation. They have the detector and a set of headphones—equipment that is not cheap. Many of them also choose a certain time of day for their excursion, and they typically work alone.

Something is interesting about those skilled treasure hunters: their slow, methodic motion. They walk and sweep and walk and sweep with their expensive devices. Then, suddenly, you can tell their metal detector just "pinged" or transmitted something, and they halt abruptly. They then remain in that exact spot, and the real work begins. Now, they work much more meticulously than before.

I was a student at Thomas O. Hopkins Middle School many years ago in Burlington Township, New Jersey. I remember during those years riding with my dad on a road called Neck Road on our way to church in Florence, New Jersey. That day, something amazing was happening. During someone's search of a wooded area, perhaps looking for an object they lost, they discovered an authentic Indian arrowhead! The artifact was hundreds of years old! Once it was officially dated and appraised, it sold for a hefty sum of money.

Naturally, overnight, there were scores of people searching those woods for more arrowheads. Amazingly, people began to find them. I recall going along with a friend and his parents to search for those artifacts. There was a sense of thrill and excitement for all who participated. Part of the fascination was the fact that somebody — anybody (even me) — might find one of those arrowheads that could be sold for a lot of money. The other part of the fun increased our adrenaline just being on the hunt. Everyone found a spot and had their own tools with which to dig. Everyone had their own bag to store their treasures in, all while imagining what they were going to do with their share of the money. Everyone did what they thought was necessary to give them the best chance to better their lives.

I never did find anything. To the best of my recollection, no one I knew found anything, either. Still, I had the thrill of the moment!

Sometimes, when hope or a dream is lost or abandoned, it's like searching for those unearthed ancient Indian arrowheads. Part of the thrill of recovering something is the adventure of doing it.

Throughout our lives, we have had many hopes and dreams. Let me describe it like this: Hopes are like veins. We know we have those little fellas streaming throughout our entire bodies. They are used to carry blood away from our hearts. In our bodies, there are also main arteries. Those are the big boys. They carry blood to the heart. You don't want to mess with those guys.

The hope I'm referring to is a major artery. It is one of those things that keep us alive. I'm talking about major artery hope in this book, but we need both veins and arteries to live. Someone may be saying, *"I understand what you mean, but I can't tell the difference between the veins* (everyday dreams) *and the arteries* (once in a lifetime hope)." Well, another word for the idea of major artery hope is passion. It is the biggest thing inside you. It is that thing you can talk about all day long. The chances are that in some capacity, you may already be doing it. Perhaps it is the thing you mimicked as a child.

My mother told me that as children, my two cousins and I would play church. One of my cousins was the deacon. My other cousin was a trustee (interestingly, the latter cousin is a very successful car dealership manager and an Elder in the church). Then, there was me. I liked to mimic the preacher. I was born to communicate.

Hope or passion is the one thing you desire to do more than anything else. It is usually the thing you will do more effectively than anything else. You will need adequate time to become comfortable doing it, and probably a little skill-sharpening, too. But once you are completely ready to step out there, it will be one of the most satisfying things in which you will ever engage!

While we're rebuilding our hope after the storm of adversity, it's a wonderful time to simplify what a storm is. A storm is an atmospheric disturbance characterized by a strong wind, usually accompanied by rain, snow, sleet, etc.

Now that we talked about what hope is and have clarified what a storm is, don't forget what we're doing with our hope after the storm: rebuilding. Again, rebuilding is repairing or remodeling something extensively by taking apart and reconstructing, often with new parts. Many times, after the storms of adversity, we must reevaluate our hopes and dreams and reconstruct them with some new parts.

There are definite similarities between adversity and a natural storm. Adversity, just like a violent storm, will cause a disturbance. It is something that interrupts the normal flow of things. Like a strong storm's wind blowing, adversity is also characterized by strong gusts of intense pressure. There is a force that is exerting pressure or opposition, trying to move you in the opposite direction.

One summer, I was visiting family out of state. It was our annual Crawford Family Reunion. That homecoming was one of the best. No event is perfect (as any planner will tell you), but there was more than enough food, and it was prepared with that southern hospitality kind of love. The facility was more than adequate with an arcade and bowling alley, which our family made perfect use of while there. What sealed the deal for me concerning the quality and thought that went into planning the gathering was this:

As I stepped outside to head over to the promenade to where they were starting the program, I felt what could be described as a huge foot kick me hard enough to leave a bruise. There was something that, in the excitement and cool satisfaction of the moment, had slipped away from the forefront of my mind: the heat! The forecast for that day was not high humidity but excessive heat. It was supposed to hit 94 degrees and had reached its goal. That caused great concern for many of us because we had parents or close relatives who were in attendance, and it would have been dangerous for them to be outside with those temperatures. We love and respect our older family members immensely.

One of the things that have always been important to my dad, his brothers, sisters, aunts, uncles, and cousins — and now, me — is the reading of the Family Tree. That meant wherever and whenever that reading would take place during the day, they would all be there — extreme heat or not. If we knew what was best for us, we would be there, too.

So, you can imagine my delight as I got closer to the promenade and realized the huge black boxes that I thought were speakers were actually air conditioners—portable, outside, and working very effectively. Fantastic!

Life is amazing sometimes. Occasionally, you're just going through the daily routine of living when out of nowhere comes a bonus piece of life in the middle of everyday life, kind of like when you make breakfast, crack open an egg, and find two yolks inside.

As I consider how adversity can resemble an atmospheric storm that causes a disruption or disturbance in the normal flow of things, I'm reminded of something else. We all received a celestial gratuity near Summerton, South Carolina, around the time of the family reunion that certainly caused a disruption in the normal flow of things.

One day, after the close of the family reunion, something spectacular happened. On Monday, August 21, 2017, at 2:31 p.m., there was a total solar eclipse! That phenomenon doesn't happen every day and was in no way planned. It just happened to be a bonus piece of life for those of us who were visiting. On the other hand, the sighting in South Carolina was one of the best in the whole country. Because of the totality of the duration (the amount of time it was the strongest and could be seen the clearest), people literally came from all over the country to see it. For those already in South Carolina or near Summerton where we were, we understood there was a clear disruption of the normal flow of things. Traffic was backed up everywhere. The news media was all over the place. People had stopped and parked their cars anywhere and everywhere for that special occasion.

Naturally, during those few moments, it was as if time stood still. Of course, me being me, I instinctively looked up into the sky just when the eclipse could be seen without any protective glasses. Then, someone stepped outside of a bank and handed me a pair. It was certainly picturesque. The whole scenario was something I'd never witnessed before. Many who had viewed an eclipse for the first time were in tears. Although that was not adversity, it certainly caused a great disturbance and disruption in South Carolina that day.

As the storm of adversity approaches, remember this warning: *"Severe storm watch in effect! Expect strong emotions."* Strong emotions can accompany adversity. Like a drenching rain, you may feel completely soaked down to your socks with discouragement at times. Like a blanketing snow, you may experience feeling cold and insensitive. Like the sting of hail or sleet pelting your skin, you may feel the sting of people's negative opinions. Also, during adversity, like thunder, you may experience the deafening emotion of anger. Like a bolt of lightning, you may give in to the surge of impulsiveness.

All those emotions and more may, at times, accompany the storms of adversity. But after the storms of adversity, we assess the damages. Then, we must take stock of ourselves. We must make up our minds that now is the time. We still have what it takes to rebuild our hope and pursue it. Don't forget: When we rebuilt, we repair and reconstruct, but we often use new parts. Those parts come from various places. They may come from people we respect. They may also come from a spiritual leader—someone who is insightful. They can come from self-education, too. As we begin to reconstruct our hope, new pieces of the puzzle will come from things we learned on our journey through adversity.

Now, let me say this: You may be someone who is already focused, which helps you progress in self-development. Maybe you don't flinch when the storms of adversity come your way. Maybe you are poised. Maybe you have the kind of determination that enables you to remain persistent in pursuit of your hope. Maybe your vision involves human needs, and that weight pulled you forward, even while you were in the storm of adversity. If so, you are probably an exceptional human being.

For the rest of us, many are still rebuilding, but we won't give up. No storm, no matter its intensity, is going to stop us. We will not take our eyes off the prize, even when it hurts. There is no quit in us. We are the graduates of the University of Adversity, and we have learned perseverance.

We live hope, and we give hope.

# Chapter Ten
# The Dream Team

Ladies and gentlemen, now introducing the **Dream Team**! Different images may arise when the phrase "Dream Team" is evoked. I think of various all-star teams in different sports. Images of players who dominated the game also come to mind. The idea I am going to attach to the term is probably different from what you are thinking.

We have come through the storms of adversity. We have assessed the damage of the storm and begun rebuilding our hope with some new parts. We are excited about moving into our destiny. Now that we have recovered and are rebuilding something valuable. We also need something very important. We need dream protection.

Everything we value, we protect. Banks have vaults. Cars have alarms. We even have firewalls set up to protect our computer's information. But what do we install in our lives to protect ourselves? Could it be that we sometimes don't appraise our own value as humans as we do "things"? Aren't you worth protecting? I sure am, and so are you.

That is the meat of this chapter. When you have hope, vision, or passion, it is wise to have other people in your life to help protect and develop your dreams — your personal Dream Team. Your Dream Team will be on board with you. They are individuals who believe in you — period. They are people who will help you accomplish your dream. They will be with you when self-discipline is fading. They will be there when you are up and when you are down. They know your dream, and they also know you. They will dream with you and become a team to which you will become accountable. That is where it gets touchy.

Many successful people don't mind having others in their lives who answer to them. However, they seem to have a conflict when they have people to whom they must answer. One of the meanings for the word accountable is answerable.

We all need to have people in our lives we answer to. They help us become better. Not just on our jobs, but in life. King Solomon wrote, *"In the multitude of counsel, there is safety."* The benefit of having another set of eyes in life is they can see what you don't. Many traumatic situations could have been averted if someone had only listened to the person trying to warn them. That's why as we move forward in life, it is wise to envision — even before we need them — a group of people who can make us better, keep us accountable, and help us protect our dream.

For me, when I consider my outlook on life, I have an interesting perspective. Twenty-five years ago, I was trapped in a world of addiction. The most intense, painful, and aggressive struggle I have had in my life by far was coming out of that. That struggle made me courageous enough to scrutinize my own soul consistently. There is no experience like waking up day after day, looking at yourself in the mirror and wondering who you have become. I thank God I never unpacked internally and settled into that awful place of being who I never wanted to be. The good part is that eventually, it planted in me a trait of relentless self-development as a way of life. For instance, I am in college at the time of this writing, getting another level of oratory skill, learning Spanish, and studying classical music. I count myself fortunate that today, it is not very difficult for me to seek guidance or counsel in an area of my life that needs coaching from my real-life Dream Team.

If it is okay, I'm going to use the game of basketball as an illustration. Examine how the following positions on a team could coincide with your Dream Team.

Just about all basketball teams have a point guard. Point guards are often responsible for directing plays and passing the ball. If we have been around basketball at all, most of us have seen that player in action. The player has probably left a lasting image in your mind with his ability to make those dazzling no-look or behind-the-back passes that seem unreal. Until you try it for yourself, you won't appreciate the fact that they also make it look so easy. The point guard's role is like that of a team's captain. That player is typically the team's best ball handler and passer.

On your Dream Team, that person will help to protect your emotional stability. They will help guard your emotional health as you soar, twist, and stretch to reach your hope and dream. When you become engrossed in the pursuit of a dream, you sometimes don't pay attention to your emotions the way you should. Your emotions are essential to your overall health, as we have already discussed. That person on your Dream Team will know you well enough to know when you are placing too much pressure on yourself or not enough. Of course, that player must be (just as all the rest of the people on your Dream Team) a person you trust and feel safe opening up your life to.

Acquiring the skill of being able to trust someone is vital to succeeding in the game of life. Many people have always had that ability. On the other hand, there are people in life (like me) who have undergone unusual and baneful circumstances. Those unhealthy events might have left you with an inability to trust others naturally. When it's hard to trust people, you should try your best to fight through that wall. There is a better you on the other side. When you trust a person to be the point guard on your Dream Team, they will add to the team by being able to give a nudge of constructive criticism from time to time. Just like the keen senses of an effective point guard on the court, that player on your team is also an invaluable piece of the puzzle. When the point guard is playing effectively, they will assist the rest of the team in being successful as well. That player can pick up on your emotional temperature.

Interestingly, it almost sounds strange for a non-mental health professional, African American male to be vocalizing the benefits of emotional well-being. That's because somewhere in our society, we have demonized the reality that people (male and female), from time to time, need an emotional tune-up. Until we overcome that misrepresentation and relabel it as humane and acceptable, we will continue to suffer as a society needlessly.

Your personal Dream Team is a support mechanism. They will support you in pursuit of your dreams. Many great people with overwhelming potential have fallen apart within and/or without because they didn't have the proper support. You must have a Dream Team to support you in pursuit of your hope. You will also need them once you fully achieve your hope, as they will serve as a force to help you stay grounded and humble.

So, the first player you need on your Dream Team is a point guard. Next, you must have a shooting guard. In many cases, a shooting guard is the team's best shooter, as is stated in its name. Typically, he or she can consistently hit long-range shots (of 20 feet or more). The shooting guard has usually earned a level of respect. One common denominator runs through most effective shooting guards: That person will shoot and shoot and shoot and shoot. It doesn't necessarily make them a ball hog (most of the time); they are just fearless. Even when a shooting guard is going through a slump, the coach usually advises the team to encourage him or her to shoot themselves out of it, which they usually do. It may take a few minutes, a game or two, a couple of weeks, or even months.

Another attribute the shooting guard usually carries is confidence. They are confident in themselves, which creates confidence that others have in them as well, especially the other teammates. Besides being able to shoot the ball, they tend to have very good ball-handling skills and the ability to drive the ball to the basket.

Basketball handling skills link together another fundamental necessity. In the curriculum of our newly opened school, "The University of Adversity," one of the core attitudes I teach is learning to cope. To cope means to handle. It's how you deal with things. Honestly, all the players on a great basketball team must be able to handle the ball. Likewise, every person on your Dream Team must have good ball-handling skills or coping skills.

The second player on your Dream Team — the shooting guard — would be your finance person. Above everyone else, they must be someone you trust (probably someone you have known for many years). They must also be a person who is proficient in what they do. First and foremost, however, they must be a person who does things right — ethically. Integrity is critical in every walk of life, and finances are no exception.

It seems like in every area of sports, revelations are surfacing about some form of cheating. It has become acceptable in many circles to do whatever they must to win. Unfortunately, that pervasive mindset in sports yields a lower level of respect and admiration for sports figures outside the arena among their fans.

Your shooting guard (finance manager) must be one who would rather not play at all than break the rules. Fiscal management and profitability are ways of keeping score. They are ways you can gauge how you are doing in your life. You must have someone on your Dream Team who knows how to score and help you keep score. The person who plays the position of finances on your team should be a "true guard" — someone who has a strong talent or gift in that area. After all, that is what they will do for you and your family: "guard" your dream.

So many professionals — athletes, entertainers, and even executives — have had their hope asphyxiated because they didn't have the right person on their team in the financial guard position. Often, people surround themselves with individuals who will agree with them in most situations because they sign the checks. That can be dangerous.

You must have someone around you who will help you guard your identity. While your hope is beginning to grow, it may seem small. You can effectively manage it at that stage, but soon, it will grow. That's when it will pay off to have your Dream Team in place.

Next, let's talk about the forward position. The small forward position is perhaps the most versatile of the main five basketball positions. Due to the nature of its role, small forwards have various weapons, such as quickness and strength inside the painted area near the basket.

You must have a person on your Dream Team playing the forward position who will also do what their title says; help the team move forward. The small forward position on your team represents public relations or a salesperson. That person will challenge you to continue to develop socially and relationally outside the team. They will help stretch the boundaries of the opportunities the team gets to play. They will help push you and the team to new levels of success. They will empower you to present your hope to diverse kinds of individuals and organizations. The small forward will help you avoid the pitfall of only connecting with those you are most comfortable with. Usually, the people we are most comfortable with are those with whom we have the most in common.

As your hope is being achieved, you will need someone to help you stay focused on spending some time developing key relationships and associations. That person on your Dream Team may have the skills to be a personal manager, mentor, or business advisor. They will push you to develop your ability to become socially skillful constantly. There may be things about your personality that need to be adjusted so that you are friendlier and more approachable. Your speech or attire may be things that make people feel you represent a specific geographic and economic status. The small forward on your team will be able to assist you in those areas while you pursue your hopes and dreams.

There is yet another important position on your team: a player called the power forward. In basketball, a power forward plays a role like that of the center on offense. They can "post up" (play with their back to the basket) or set up for mid-range jump shots. On defense, they play under the basket in a zone defense or against the opposing power forward. Up until now, I have not really mentioned defense, but it is important. The power forward position is vital on defense because they play in the middle in a zone defense and protect the basket. There will always be an opposing team out there somewhere. Someone on the team must be aware of the opposing team and be bold enough to challenge their attempts at approaching the basket. If that person is not skillful and aggressive, it will be a challenge trying to win games.

Many people, having achieved their hope, forgot, or never considered the power forward as an important part of their Dream Team. That player is the health or physical fitness guru. They have an interest in your health and the health of other teammates as well. The physical demands and obligations that are placed on an individual or team that has an aggressive pursuit of a goal can be intense. You must do your best to stay in decent shape. That is a tall order.

When you say, *"Get in shape,"* many people just consider exercise, which is a very important factor. However, there are at least two other vital components to a person's overall health. It is just as important to have a healthy diet. Eating right is one area of our lives that, with a little practice, can easily become a habit. However, it is a wall that is not so easily broken initially because many of us have not had the greatest eating habits for so long that unhealthy eating has become our way of life. Exercise and proper diet are the core of having good health.

The third area we must be aware of is getting proper rest. Many people don't realize how important it is to get six to eight hours of sleep a day. When we sleep, our bodies literally restore and replenish themselves. When your body is rested, it is like a car that has just had a tune-up and oil change. It is now able to perform with all the power it has at its disposal. The immune system is also more prone to function optimally when we receive the proper amount of sleep. Our hope cannot be achieved if we are physically unable to attain it.

That is the value of having the right person playing that power forward (health) position. We sometimes need that extra push. We need someone who is as concerned (if not moreso) about our waistline than the bottom line. We need a player on our team who won't let us cross the line and burn ourselves out or injure ourselves by demanding a unrealistic workload. To be a workaholic today in many circles is the norm. With so much emphasis on staying competitive and greed, some have become so consumed by their passion, they overlook how they are treating themselves.

The power forward will help us to watch our physical fitness so that we can chase that hope, dream, or passion effectively. That may also mean placing the dream on hold temporarily if serious medical attention is needed. An accurate observation from that player on the team could be the difference between life or death. Remember: You and I give steam to the dream! The quality and quantity of the steam depend largely on our well-being.

One more player is needed for our Dream Team to make it complete: a strong center or "big man/big woman in the middle." The center usually plays near the baseline, close to the basket. The tallest player is most likely to be assigned to the position of center. As one of the tallest players on the team, the center will have the most precise view of the floor, usually scores "down low, in the paint," and can be a good perimeter shooter. They can draw good rebounds and have the skill to score close to the basket.

The person who plays the center position is the spiritual player on your Dream Team. The importance of that person cannot be overstated. I believe visionaries can have stability and longevity if they can manage to stay spiritually connected. My definition of spirituality has to do with God, Jesus, and the Holy Bible. Yours may be different, but spirituality should include the reality of accessing a force that can empower, encourage, and provide guidance in times when the way is not clear, and no other human being has an adequate resolution. They should be someone who can add something that supersedes your humanness. If you do not consider yourself to be that kind of person, it is all the more reason why the center on your team is invaluable to you. They will help point you in the direction of spiritual significance and success.

Now, I know there are scores of people who won't believe spirituality has anything to do with the rest of the team. I understand that, and we will just agree to disagree.

When things are going great, we sometimes tend to relax and let our guard down. That is also the time when some who may not have our best interest at heart may approach us. We all need someone on our team who cannot be lured away from their values in times of great financial success.

Well, that makes up your Dream Team, more or less. Even though I have used players from a basketball team to illustrate the kind of support you can have, it was used to serve as an example. Your team can have five players supporting you or 50, but on the team, the goal is yours. The people on your team will help you reach your hope or dream, but you will set the pace. You will drive the team—your Dream Team.

## Chapter Eleven
## Grown-Up Hope Is A Realized Dream

Have you ever planted a seed? You watch each day and finally see that first tiny little green sprout breaking through the soil. It's amazing! Then, you notice one or two more blades and a little flower budding. I can't explain it, but to observe the process is somehow calmly incredible.

I remember vaguely, as do many of you, those little milk cartons from years ago. I don't recall the name of the brand, but some of you may. I just remember they were white with green writing on them. If I recall correctly, it was tomato or string bean seeds we planted. I remember being given my seeds from the teacher. Anxiously, I grabbed my seed packet. I couldn't wait to plant my seeds in my little milk carton, complete with my name on it. That was in the first or second grade, so none of us really had a clue what was going to happen next. I do remember practically running to class the very next day to observe my plant's progress. Much to my surprise, there was absolutely nothing happening. Most of the kids, including myself, were shattered. One girl was crying. It was a moment of little people pandemonium!

I suppose when I think about it now, we must have thought it was magic or something. That was back during the whole "Jack and the Beanstalk" era. At some point, the teacher must have realized she left out some critical information. She sat us all down and explained a little more what the process would be like. It must have sunk in that time because I remember that I wasn't really bothered by the fact that I saw no visible vegetation over the next three or four days. When some of the other kids began to see some progress with their seed, it was day five, and I still had no greenery.

Okay. Where's my teacher? **Conference on the mound!!!**

*"One more day, and then we will have to replant,"* she said.

Replant?! I remember thinking on the way to school, *"Someone is playing some kind of trick with my seed!"*

Well, as I walked in the class and over to the window ledge, looking into my little white carton, I thought, *"Wow! There it is!"* Sticking halfway out of the dirt was a little green doubled-over stem and a little leaf. ***"I DID IT!"*** I yelled. My teacher just smiled.

The moral of the story here is this: When you take time to observe and appreciate your own progress, you will have a similar kind of experience. Initially, your hope or dream is just that—a dream, a seed. It is something that is just a concept that remains in the mind of one person: you! You must act. Do something! Take some action. Once you do, your dream begins its process of realization.

A seed on a shelf at the hardware store simply can never grow. You must grab those seeds and plant them. You must act. Do something!

Don't get me wrong. I'm all for planning and strategizing. However, I also know it can become all too easy to fall into a cycle of procrastination. Let me take a moment to reiterate some facts about fear. As you reach the time of acting on your dream or hope, you will encounter a series of fears. Those fears speak to us and try to convince us of things like:

*"That will never work."*

*"Others better than you have tried that, and they've failed. What if you fail?*

*"You don't have enough experience to succeed at this."*

*"What will people say?"*

We must confront fear. First, say, *"Fear, why wouldn't it work? I have worked hard, got good advice, and even received prayer. It will work!"*

Secondly, you can respond with, *"If I do fail at first, I still won't give up. I just keep learning more."*

Sometimes, you must fail a few times before you succeed.

In baseball, you usually get a strike before you get a hit. I don't need to hit every ball, just the ones I'm supposed to hit. Years ago, I was in sales. They taught me about the law of averages. There was only a certain amount of *"Nos"* I would get before I got a *"Yes."* So, I learned not only to accept the nos but also to get excited about them, realizing that every passing no brought me closer to a yes.

Next, tell fear, *"Just because I don't have a lot of experience doesn't mean I have to fail. I am willing to learn and have a tremendous amount of desire."*

Lastly, tell fear, *"People will talk whether I do this or not, so people's commentary about me can't move me."*

You will never see your hope begin to grow if you cannot overcome fear. Not so long ago, I was reminded of an excellent acronym for fear. Fear stands for:

<u>F</u>alse
<u>E</u>vidence
<u>A</u>ppearing
<u>R</u>eal

Some acronyms seem like people just had some time on their hands, so they made an acronym. That one, however, is different. It is awesome and so very accurate. Fear really is false evidence. The dark voice you hear will never be able to offer proof to back its claim because, quite simply, there is none. At the same time, you must recognize it appears real, but it's not.

Once you have uncovered and rebuilt your hope and start to act on it, you must regularly work with your dream. Most plants need sunlight, water, and good soil. Your hopes and dreams also need certain elements to keep them growing.

## *Enthusiasm*

Stay excited about your own dream. After all, it is yours. Once you get started, you should speak with excitement to others about your new hope. Never let someone dampen your dream because they will try. You cannot expect others to get excited about something that you are not. Your attitude about your new hope will be contagious, whether it's good or not so good.

We are fast to jump and celebrate other people's accomplishments. We should be the same way about our own, especially when we look back over the many obstacles we have hurdled to reach that special place.

I have been working on this literary project for five years, and it is my very first. Once this book is published, I am going to celebrate like I just won an Oscar!

Your dream needs your enthusiasm!

## *Knowledge*

Knowledge, training, and mentorship are hope food. You must keep practicing to perfect what you have. Read, attend lectures and seminars, and build relationships with people who are successfully doing what you want to do. Push yourself to keep developing. You can't get satisfied after your first success, or your hope will begin to die. Keep blazing a path. Always look to add more and more to yourself. Once you have planted the seed of our dream by acting on it, you will then see it begin to grow. Then, plant some more and repeat the process. Soon, you will have a garden of greatness. Make full use of your time.

I almost forgot: You must always make sure the condition of your soil is the best. That means paying attention to where your dream or hope is planted. Obviously, if it has grown and is alive today, the place you originally planted it was good soil. However, over time, soil composition changes. Businesses change, relationships change, buying trends change, geographical demands change, and people (including ourselves) change. All those things adjust over time, so it is imperative that you monitor their quality. Be willing to launch out in a new direction if it becomes evident something is no longer yielding the positive results it once did.

Lastly, just like a young plant, you must be willing to protect your dream from certain elements. It is not practiced as much today as it was years ago, but there was a time when in every field or crop, you were sure to see a scarecrow, and scared crows it did—along with rabbits, opossums, chickens, and probably a small child or two.

Extreme heat, pests, drought, and weeds can destroy some plants. Many things will attempt to destroy your dreams, but you must be proactive in protecting them. The greatest weapon you have against the enemies of hope is your mind. You must win the battle in your mind first. See yourself advancing with your hope intact. Imagine the kinds of things your hope will produce in you and others. Make it as personal as you can. Imagine your face, body, and entire being succeeding and obtaining the hope you are expecting. Use your words and thoughts as pesticides against the weeds that try to grow alongside your dreams. Stay at it long enough, and I promise your dream will grow—and so will you.

Let me take a second to reach back into the last chapter and grab a principle that applies here. Once you begin to see your hope's growth and success, it is vital to stay connected to the right people—your Dream Team. Why? Because they will help you stay rooted and grounded.

In other words, the right people will help you stay humble, no matter how successful you become. Keep a few people around you who seem to always have a stickpin in their hand and are not afraid to use it. They are professional bubble-busters. They won't attack you in a degrading or disrespectful way, but they are not afraid to say what needs to be said, sometimes more than once! Just when you imagine your plant of hope has grown two whole feet, they'll measure it and tell you, *"Nope. It's just two inches."* Those people are invaluable.

It is very important to write your dreams, visions, and hopes down and date them. Be flexible. Growth is measurable. The best way to measure a goal's progress is by writing it down and then, a short time later, go back to the original plan and see how it has developed.

That reminds me of checking the growth of a seed you planted, but here's the difference: Once you plant a few seeds, you must make sure the conditions are right. The seeds will pretty much grow on their own. On the other hand, your hope will not grow by itself. It will take massive amounts of time, sweat, thinking, and planning, which may be the most challenging thing you have ever taken upon yourself. Still, if you persevere (as you have already agreed you would), it will be worth it.

Okay. You have taken your seed off the shelf, opened its package, courageously planted it, and it has begun to grow. For your hope and vision to be realized, you and it must weather the storm. But how do you really know if your hope is realized? How can you tell if your dream tree has matured or not? There are many answers to those questions.

Some would say "income," meaning that you have arrived once you have achieved a certain level of profitability. Others might say it is "recognition." In other words, you can really gauge a person's accomplishments by who knows them and their work, or that their name is mentioned along with other great names. Both are legitimate measures of success, but I would like to add one other concept mentioned previously.

What do you think is the greatest potential within a single tree? I think it is more trees. What do I mean? Well, there are actually many trees in one. How can that be, you ask? That's very simple. A tree has a very special dynamic built into it. It can produce itself through its seed. For an Oak tree, it's called an acorn. A tree can produce many hundreds of acorns over its lifetimes. Each one has the potential to grow on its own, but many will not produce other trees. Only a few will.

Many of our trees—hopes, dreams, and visions—will never produce other trees, either. A select few will become full trees. A vital component of a full-grown hope, dream, or vision is that it can give birth to other hopes, dreams, or visions. Your hope should plant seeds or inspiration in others, empowering them to pursue their dreams. That idea should prompt us to look within.

What are our lives producing in the lives of others? What acorns are falling from our trees? Or have we become so selfish, we don't have the slightest concern about anything benefiting others?

I suggest if the only thing we measure our dream's full stature by is our own satisfaction, we may be considered shallow failures on the scale of the betterment of humanity. I believe your hope is full-grown when your dream is achieved, and when your dream is achieved, it should plant in others the seeds to dream their own dream and hope in their own hope.

# Chapter Twelve
# Just Can't Imagine

It's time to wrap it up! We have talked about many ideas that you may have already been familiar with. Hopefully, it's likely I just added a different nuance to some concepts you have already grasped. It is possible, though, you still feel like you need a little more hope but didn't really find it in this book. Sometimes, the place we thought we would find an answer turns out to be an experience that leaves us still searching.

Many years ago, I was in an extreme financial bind. I thought maybe there was some kind of "get rich quick scheme" out there that I had not come across yet in my life. I secretly sought out that magical financial elixir on the late-night infomercial circuit, looking for something I could theoretically digest and, in effect, transform my whole financial world. I envisioned myself jogging on a white sandy beach within a matter of weeks without a care in the world. I could have a beautiful mansion with two or three luxury cars parked in their own separate garages. A personal chef who would prepare the most exotic dishes made to my liking would reside in my home. Those ideas and more swirled in my head during that short period in my mid-twenties.

Surely, you recall those commercials that would come on television, quickly hijacking our imagination during your younger years. *"You can have this,"* they'd say. *"You can drive that and live here,"* they teased. Then, there was always, *"You never knew you could have this great, big old truckload of cash if you just spent this little teeny-weeny amount of time doing this. I can show you how!"*

When you are a trifecta—young, immature, and in debt—you think, *"Yes! This is what I've been looking for!"* For me, that magic potion was real estate. I knew I could buy low and sell high or, if I wanted to, invest with no money down. *"Why use my own money to get rich when I don't have to? That's brilliant!"* I mused, especially since I didn't have any money of my own. So, I found someone who had one of those "no money down real estate investment packages" that they didn't mind letting me borrow. Suffice it to say, real estate is and can be a very viable, lucrative investment—when used responsibly by a wise and disciplined individual.

Two concepts seemed never to be able to access my gated mind once I started consuming that magic real estate elixir. First, if the guy who had the program was giving it to me, why wasn't he running on a white sandy beach with blue water himself? Secondly, the glaring reason I got into all that mess from the start (my irresponsibility) had not changed and would only repeat itself in the new endeavor, if not altered. There was nothing wrong with the information; it was just missing a live human being to go with it. I would have needed an actual tour guide to navigate that journey, which was not included with the package. Rather disappointingly, I was left feeling emptier and more hopeless after drinking the magic potion than I was before.

Maybe you think your situation is similar. You feel as if you are in a hopeless situation, even after making sincere attempts to change it. There is one thing I find mind-boggling as I reflect on my own firsthand experiences. I can now look back and see that for so many years, I was going through major pain, fear, and maybe even depression, but I just kept it all inside. Now, I must say that I had been assessed by my social science professor years ago as being an introvert, but that still doesn't quite explain away my choice to hold all of those things inside that I later discovered were toxic.

It's interesting to me that even in our most sincere attempts to break through hopeless situations, we often don't share the nature of our struggles with others. The English word "hopeless" is, in itself, interesting as well. It is obviously a derivative of our root word, **HOPE**. Hopeless means "having no expectation of or showing no sign of a favorable outcome." A hopeless situation also means "impossible to solve or deal with."

You may have lost a loved one or are facing the awkward challenges of a dysfunctional relationship. Perhaps you have lost a decent job or have experienced a recent foreclosure on a home. You might feel the situation you are currently in is hopeless. You just can't imagine a favorable outcome.

The good news is this: **YOUR SITUATION IS NOT HOPELESS!** It is not impossible to solve!

In studying situations where people felt they wanted to end their life, one of the main causes was the deep sense of hopelessness often found in depression. People have concluded there is no way whatsoever there would be a favorable outcome. That deep sense of hopelessness, combined with an inadequate ability to resolve conflict, is also a root cause of homicide. It may also be that some people just need a different perspective, indicating that something serious needs to change.

In our humanness, we sometimes don't adequately utilize one of our body's most essential components: the mind. Think about it. We have been intelligently designed! I believe many of our problems (not all) can be solved if we would just get mad enough to no longer accept no for an answer and be determined enough to search every resource at our disposal. We have intellect and ingenuity, but at times, we struggle with having real power to direct our thoughts in productive ways.

That is a skill we must master to reach our goals, hopes, and dreams—a skill that seems to come easier for some than others. I suppose I was one of the "others." There were times in my life when I had a major conflict with my own thoughts. It was, in fact, a civil war: Me vs. Me.

One of the things about our thought life that is so amazing is this: Whether good or bad, strong or weak, the thoughts we experience at any given moment seem very real, even if they are not. Some people have undergone traumatic experiences in their lives, and like an old sweater that shrank over time, they just seem to outgrow it. It almost seems as though after a few years pass, they simply realize, *"This doesn't fit me anymore."* So, they take that pain, hang it on a coat rack, and go about their merry way, never looking back.

I have several good friends who have had that experience in their lives. That always fascinates me. If I'm honest—and I am—I get just a tad bit envious occasionally. When I look at certain portions of my life, some things become vividly clear. During a time that I spent far away from Burlington Township, New Jersey, my lifestyle and attitude, as well as many of those around me, seemed to be that of joyriding on a high-speed rail line on the way to a stop called "Self-Destruction." There is absolutely no doubt in my mind that for one reason and one alone, I did not ride that train to one of its usual ends—prison, six feet under, mental deficiency, or chronic illness. The reason is simple: I had a mother who refused to give up on me and who refused to stop praying for me.

So, for all those hopeless situations where you have tried everything you know to change, all to no avail, make sure you have not settled on hopelessness until you have given God a try. The Bible says that He can be a friend that is closer than a brother.

I started this book by sharing with you an actual experience I had while riding the subway. It was all too real. I described it as a portrait because that is how it seemed to me at the time; a portrait that was alive. With words, I painted a portrait of a situation that can seem very hopeless for many: addiction and co-dependency — one person caught in the bear trap of drug addiction, while the other (who was obviously a non-drug user) is caught in the bear trap of love and dedication to the addict, emotionally handcuffed.

I have counseled enough girlfriends, mothers, and siblings of those intertwined with loved ones who were entangled with drugs or alcohol to understand how futile it can seem even to try to muster up enough hope to believe that person can ever change. At times, I am fascinated by the experience because, while trying to insist to those loving people that if the right kind of tough love can be administered by them, accompanied by an intervention — and with God's help — that person can be free.

I am also holding up my own life as proof and a trophy cup of what God can do. So, although addiction and co-dependency can seem like the pinnacle of hopelessness, know that still, there is hope. We must resolve for ourselves or a loved one that quitting is not an option. They and we can never give up on the hope that someday, somehow, something will happen that will make a difference.

We **CAN**…
We **MUST**…
*Overcome our Storms and Rebuild our Hope!*

## About the Author

**R**odney Bennett has resided in New Jersey for most of his life. He is a proud graduate of Burlington Township High School. Over the years, he has studied at Burlington County College, Philadelphia College of the Bible, and, at the time of this writing, seeking a degree from Victory Education Training Institute and Bible College. He is presently employed at Purato's, Inc. in Pennsauken, New Jersey.

Rodney's most tumultuous times occurred during his youth, from the ages of 10 through 19. During those years, he found himself entangled with some of the most deadly assassins in the world. At age 11, nicotine; age 13, alcohol; age 14, introduced to marijuana; by age 15, nightclubs and the "streets"; age 16, cocaine; age 17, street hustling and promiscuity; by the age of 23, he was known as "Rock" and became addicted to drugs.

Several years later, through the prompting of his mother, he was introduced to Rev. Wayne Holmes. Rev. Holmes was a Pastor and Prison Chaplain who became a friend, counselor, and mentor who trained Rodney in spiritual warfare and how to triumph over adversity. That was the beginning of many extraordinary years spent matriculating through the University of Adversity.

By God's grace, successfully defeating those destiny killers has forged Rodney's success, determination, and expertise in Overcoming Adversity and Rebuilding Hope. Over the past 25 years, speaking to audiences of various cultures, age groups, and social backgrounds has shown Rodney to be an exciting, effective, and personable communicator and Hope Rebuilder. Experienced in various settings, including schools, churches, conference centers, and businesses, this Preacher and

Motivational Speaker has been well received. In today's unprecedented times of hopelessness and despair, new doors of opportunity open all the time for this exceptional presenter.

The University of Adversity is a unique learning institution that offers a new breed of **HOPE**! It is the platform where Rodney's new venture as Speaker and Author is being launched.

*"Reasons to quit are everywhere you look.
HUNT for reasons not to!"*
**~ Rodney Bennett ~**

**Motivate — Elevate — Educate … RodneyBSpeaks!**

*Book him today!*

Connect with him on the web at:
www.rodneybspeaks.com

Email him at:
rodneybspeaks@gmail.com

www.ingramcontent.com/pod-product-compliance
Lightning Source LLC
Chambersburg PA
CBHW072028110526
44592CB00012B/1423